OFFSHORE
INVESTING
MADE E-Z

Arnold S. Goldstein, Ph.D.

MADE E-Z PRODUCTS, Inc.
Deerfield Beach, Florida / www.MadeE-Z.com

NOTiCE:

THIS PRODUCT IS NOT INTENDED TO PROVIDE LEGAL ADVICE. IT CONTAINS
GENERAL INFORMATION FOR EDUCATIONAL PURPOSES ONLY. PLEASE CONSULT
AN ATTORNEY IN ALL LEGAL MATTERS. THIS PRODUCT WAS NOT NECESSARILY
PREPARED BY A PERSON LICENSED TO PRACTICE LAW IN THIS STATE.

Offshore Investing Made E-Z™
©2000 Made E-Z Products, Inc.
Printed in the United States of America
MADE E-Z
PRODUCTS
384 South Military Trail
Deerfield Beach, FL 33442
Tel. 954-480-8933
Fax 954-480-8906
http://www.MadeE-Z.com/

1 2 3 4 5 6 7 8 9 10   CPC   R 10 9 8 7 6 5 4 3 2

This publication is designed to provide accurate and authoritative information in
regard to subject matter covered. It is sold with the understanding that neither the
publisher nor author is engaged in rendering legal, accounting, or other professional
services. If legal advice or other expert assistance is required, the services of a
competent professional should be sought. From: *A Declaration of Principles jointly
adopted by a Committee of the American Bar Association and a Committee of
Publishers.*

Offshore Investing Made E-Z™
Arnold S. Goldstein, Ph.D.

Important Notice

Limited warranty and disclaimer

This self-help product is intended to be used by the consumer for his/her own benefit. It may not be reproduced in whole or in part, resold or used for commercial purposes without written permission from the publisher. In addition to copyright violations, the unauthorized reproduction and use of this product to benefit a second party may be considered the unauthorized practice of law.

This product is designed to provide authoritative and accurate information in regard to the subject matter covered. However, the accuracy of the information is not guaranteed, as laws and regulations may change or be subject to differing interpretations. Consequently, you may be responsible for following alternative procedures, or using material or forms different from those supplied with this product. It is strongly advised that you examine the laws of your state before acting upon any of the material contained in this product.

As with any matter, common sense should determine whether you need the assistance of an attorney. We urge you to consult with an attorney, qualified estate planner, or tax professional, or to seek any other relevant expert advice whenever substantial sums of money are involved, you doubt the suitability of the product you have purchased, or if there is anything about the product that you do not understand including its adequacy to protect you. Even if you are completely satisfied with this product, we encourage you to have your attorney review it.

Neither the author, publisher, distributor nor retailer are engaged in rendering legal, accounting or other professional services. Accordingly, the publisher, author, distributor and retailer shall have neither liability nor responsibility to any party for any loss or damage caused or alleged to be caused by the use of this product.

Copyright Notice

The purchaser of this guide is hereby authorized to reproduce in any form or by any means, electronic or mechanical, including photocopying, all forms and documents contained in this guide, provided it is for non-profit, educational or private use. Such reproduction requires no further permission from the publisher and/or payment of any permission fee.

The reproduction of any form or document in any other publication intended for sale is prohibited without the written permission of the publisher. Publication for nonprofit use should provide proper attribution to Made E-Z Products.

Table of contents

Introduction to Offshore Investing Made E-Z™

How this book will help you

Welcome to the wonderful world of offshore finance.

In just a few hours of easy reading, you will discover how you can invest, bank and do business in hundreds of fascinating places around the world. Places where you can begin to experience a new financial freedom—one that you never knew existed . . . certainly not in today's America, and even less so in the America of tomorrow where financial freedom as we once knew it will be but a faded memory.

Against this dim reality of a lost financial freedom, more and more Americans, as well as oppressed nationals of other major countries, are taking advantage of the more liberal and enlightened laws of other nations. These nations offer financial exiles greater privacy, more wealth protection and fewer taxes than their home country does. These are the so-called offshore havens.

Once you understand what *Offshore Investing Made E-Z* can do for you, you will see that it is entirely possible to live, work, invest and do business without paying one dime in taxes to any government. You will soon learn that offshore havens can completely protect your assets from lawsuits, creditors, the IRS, ex-spouses and others anxious to put your wealth in their pockets. You will fully enjoy a sense of security in offshore havens unachievable through more conventional onshore asset protection strategies that are frequently ineffective.

Financial privacy? Face the facts. Your finances are now an open book. There's very little that big brother, or the legions of other busy-bodies and snoops, don't know about you or can't easily find out. But it need not be that way. You'll see how wealth offshore means wealth absolutely invisible to others. You, and you alone, know what you are worth. And only you will know where your wealth is located. Isn't that how it should be?

You also may believe, as I do, that you can no longer entrust your accumulation of wealth to the whims of one nation's economy. Even the wealthiest countries experience devastating economic shakeouts with their rich suddenly becoming poor. That's why I will explain to you the advantages of global investing. Hedge your bets. Reap unique investment opportunities previously unavailable to you. Become that international profiteer!

Yes, I will show you how to achieve all this—avoid taxes, gain privacy, protect your assets, and invest internationally. In summary, *Offshore Investing Made E-Z* educates you achieve a new financial freedom for you and your family. Here, in this book, are the keys to the financial advantages you want and deserve.

My goal is to open your eyes to these new offshore opportunities. You may not take advantage of each possibility, but any offshore involvement can significantly improve your financial future. Nevertheless, keep an open mind to each and every opportunity. There's little mystery surrounding offshore havens. An offshore haven is simply a country with more lenient financial and banking laws or a more favorable economy than your own. It's no longer a matter of burying your money on some tiny, remote Caribbean island. While many havens are small, emerging countries, any country can be an offshore haven to a national of another country—if it offers more attractive legal and economic features.

So let's get started.

To truly benefit from this book you must first set aside several common misconceptions about offshore havens.

Offshore havens are no longer only for the wealthy. If you have any surplus wealth to bank or invest, you owe it to yourself to check out the offshore advantage. If you pay more taxes than you think you should or have any assets worth protecting, you must "think" offshore. Many wage earners and middle class people now invest offshore. They are not millionaires, and most never will be. Yet, offshore havens perfectly suit their financial objectives, and those of millions of other ordinary people who are considered mainstream Americans.

It is not illegal to exploit offshore havens. It's your money. As an American, you can freely invest wherever you want. This is a freedom unknown to many foreigners. Yes, there are some reporting requirements when you send money offshore, and it is illegal to use havens to evade taxes, but breaking the law is not the goal of this book. I will explain how to operate offshore legally. As with most matters, there's a right way and a wrong way. Tax evaders, money launderers, drug lords and other gangsters long associated with offshore havens have perpetuated the myth that offshore banking invariably means illegal activity. But this need not be so. Hundreds of billions of dollars are legally invested overseas by law-abiding Americans. You can be one more who joins their ranks.

Offshore banking is not too difficult or too costly! You can bank, invest and do business overseas as easily as within the United States. In many respects it is even easier to bank or invest offshore. It is not complicated to set up your own company and do business offshore or set up an offshore asset protection trust. The cost of gaining the offshore advantage is usually minimum compared to the possible rewards.

Those considering offshore banking typically seek answers to many questions:

- Are some offshore havens better than others? How do you choose the right one?
- How do you select an offshore bank?
- How do you secretly move money offshore?
- What are numbered accounts?

- Must you report your offshore account to the government? To creditors?
- How safe is your money offshore?
- How do you get your money back into the country?
- How do you make deposits and withdrawals?
- Must you pay taxes on income earned offshore?
- How do you set up offshore to protect your money in the event you are sued?

These are the practical, straightforward questions this book will answer.

Offshore Investing Made E-Z will not drown you in overly technical or legal explanations (that's why you have accountants and lawyers), but it will give you a broad, simple-to-understand overview of offshore havens so you can grasp the big picture and easily translate these powerful offshore opportunities to your own situation.

Eventually you will need professional advice to safely guide you on your offshore financial adventure. While this book gives you the fundamentals on why and how you can exploit offshore havens, it also helps you to better select and work more intelligently with your advisors to achieve your goals and turn your plans into a successful reality.

Offshore Investing Made E-Z does not promote "get-rich-quick" schemes or illegal activities. Although I believe many of our laws are inequitable, archaic and oppressive, it is still always smartest to work within the law. The price you pay is simply too great when you do otherwise.

Fortunately, there are countless ways to benefit from offshore havens—without breaking one law! That is the path we shall follow.

Offshore Investing Made E-Z focuses on the four main reasons most people put their money offshore:

- Financial privacy
- Tax avoidance
- Asset protection
- International investing

Besides covering these key objectives in the first section of the book, you also will learn how to bank offshore, sidestep the offshore myths, and, most importantly, how to get started and succeed! The second section profiles the most important offshore havens and their geography, economics, politics, legal structure and the key features and advantages of greatest interest to foreign investors. It will help you to quickly identify those havens that best suit your objectives. I have worked with scores of Americans and other nationals who are now global investors. In this small way, I have shared their joy in finding a new financial freedom. My frustration is that so many Americans continue to ignore or overlook the offshore experience.

That's why I wrote this book.

Perhaps someday I'll be able to urge you to move your money back to America. It is a message I would carry with considerably more enthusiasm. As a proud American, I sincerely wish for that day. Every book reflects its author's perspective. Mine is no different.

I have been an asset protection and tax lawyer for 30 years, and it's from that perspective that I mastered the offshore game. But before you invest, I encourage you to seek other points of view by reading some of the good books listed in the Source and Resource section in the Appendix. Read on! Learn! But most of all, act . . . and take that important first step to financial freedom!

Arnold S. Goldstein, Ph.D.
Deerfield Beach, Florida

Debunking the myths

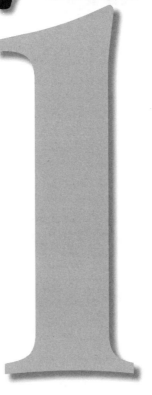

Chapter 1

Debunking
the myths

You may be one of the millions of Americans who are completely hoodwinked by the IRS . . . our bankers . . . and countless others who, for their own self-serving reasons, perpetuate the myth and lies about offshore banking. Doesn't everyone believe that offshore havens are evil, dangerous or illegal?

The fact is that most of America has been duped and deceived by this deliberate avalanche of distortions—even outright lies—about offshore havens. Consequently, most Americans have absolutely no idea what offshore banking is all about. Instead, they believe what they read or hear from a controlled media that paints offshore havens as a hangout for tax evaders, money launderers and assorted crooks and scofflaws. Uninformed lawyers, accountants and financial planners still advise their clients that offshore havens are illegal, too risky, or otherwise unworthy of consideration. They should know better—but don't!

> **note** The mystique, fear, negativity and plain ignorance that surround the concept of offshore havens is largely the result of misinformation.

Those who condemn offshore banking, and even those who promote it, seldom truly understand how these havens work. They know even less about how Americans can benefit from using them intelligently.

Of course, we can't expect the truth about offshore banking from the IRS or our U.S. banking establishment. They know that every dollar you invest offshore is one less dollar they can confiscate, control or exploit. It's easy to understand why our government and our banking and investment industries so eagerly and falsely defame and condemn offshore havens. They consistently perpetuate the myth that honest Americans don't put their money beyond our own shores. Nothing could be further from the truth.

> **HINT** Take a lesson from our own government, bankers and other financial institutions who do not follow their own advice and increasingly put their own money offshore.

But, our misunderstanding and confusion about offshore havens are not always the result of deliberate distortions. The large-scale use of offshore havens by Americans is relatively new. The tidal wave of U.S. funds to safer, more profitable lands only began in the early 1970's. Two decades of flirting with these friendly money havens makes us relative newcomers to the global money game. As amateurs, our confusion is understandable.

Contrary to what we think about ourselves, we Americans are insular people. Surrounded by two broad oceans, we are less comfortable with international dealings than are Londoners, Parisians, Berliners and other nationals who live at the crossroads of international trade and finance. Only now are we truly joining the international marketplace. In the process, we must now acclimate ourselves to how others have done business for centuries.

The mystery that clouded offshore havens is clearing slowly. We are becoming more enlightened. We are learning. This and other books help as do the many journals, newsletters, seminars and even college courses on offshore banking and international finance that are awakening America to the financial opportunities abroad. Our attitudes about offshore banking are changing gradually. We no longer blindly believe everything we see and hear about offshore havens, especially the repeated myths of the past. We are learning much about offshore banking that is good and forward-thinking. These are the financial strategies that will put us in the global economic mainstream. This is where we belong, where we can compete and prosper.

> *note*
> With this new knowledge, we will no longer be captives of the self-serving American establishment, with its own vested interests in discouraging overseas competition for your money!

Unfortunately, too many Americans still have not taken the time, nor made the effort, to discover these offshore opportunities. Perhaps, until now, you were one of them. If so, you can't hope to appreciate how offshore havens can help you unless you first shed the deep-rooted myth that offshore havens can only hurt you.

> **STRATEGY**
> To accept what is positive about offshore banking, you must clear your mind of the negative.

That's what we will do in this first chapter.

What is an offshore haven?

To take the mystery out of offshore havens, first we must define it. Only then can you clearly understand it. An *offshore haven* is simply a country other than your own. To an American, an offshore haven is anywhere you bank or invest outside the United States. If you are a Canadian, any foreign land beyond Canada is an offshore haven.

DEFINITION

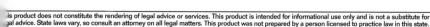

Any nation, other than your own, satisfies the definition of an offshore haven. Successful havens feature those big financial or legal benefits and outdo other countries that compete to attract international funds.

Why invest in offshore havens rather than your own country? Because, as you will see throughout this book, when you invest outside your own country, you are no longer tied to its restrictive laws, but instead enjoy the more lenient, advantageous laws of another country—laws that allow you to better accomplish one or more important financial objectives.

> **note** In financial terms, a foreign jurisdiction can only attract funds from citizens of other countries if it provides financial or legal benefits that are unavailable at home.

The fact is that whatever your financial situation, offshore havens can alleviate many financial problems that plague millions of Americans, as well as citizens of most other major countries with similarly restrictive financial laws. Chiefly, through offshore banking you can better:

- protect wealth from lawsuits and creditors

- obtain financial privacy and secrecy

- avoid, reduce or defer income and estate taxes

- invest more profitably

Of course, there are many other reasons to invest or do business overseas. For instance, American industries are rapidly moving offshore where they are less regulated and can operate more easily and profitably. Others establish captive insurance or leasing companies in offshore havens that encourage their activities with advantageous laws. Flight capital is leaving America because too many Americans see the U.S. economy as too weak to insure long-term stability. The reasons to put your money offshore are indeed endless as you will agree once you've read about the vast offshore opportunities in later chapters.

Offshore havens come in every size, variety and political persuasion. And they can be found everywhere. Bermuda, British Virgin Islands and the Bahamas hug America's southeast coast. The Cayman Islands, Turks and Caicos, Nevis and Antigua dot the Caribbean. The Isle of Man and the Channel Islands of Jersey, Guernsey and Sark shadow England. Switzerland, Liechtenstein, Luxembourg, Hungary and Austria are key European havens. The Philippines, Singapore and Hong Kong in the Far East serve the Pacific rim and exemplify the haven's geographic diversity. Clusters of havens can be found in every hemisphere and are proximate to all industrialized nations with plenty of money and arcane laws that force their citizens to find friendlier places for their wealth. And they do. The Japanese may seek Singapore or Hong Kong as havens, as Americans prefer the nearness of the Bahamas and the Caymans. But the world is shrinking fast and the choice of a haven is no longer based entirely on distance.

> **EZ TIP**
>
> We now put our money wherever our financial objectives are best met. In an age of electronic banking, this can easily be in another hemisphere as well as next door.

And contrary to another common myth, not all havens are tiny, sun-swept islands or shaky third-world countries. Switzerland, Bulgaria and Luxembourg are three havens with centuries-long traditions for taking care of depositors. The United States is considered an excellent haven because it offers foreigners considerable tax breaks to invest here. Of course, these tax breaks are unavailable to U.S. citizens. That partly explains why SO much Middle-Eastern and Japanese investment capital flows into the United States. The favorable exchange rate and the foreign view that America is a bargain-hunter's paradise add to the lustre. New and more competitive havens constantly emerge: Gibraltar, the Cook Islands, Nevis, the Marianas, Belize, Vanuatu, the Turks and

Montserrat are a few jurisdictions that only recently decided to actively compete for foreign currency. They did this by becoming very user-friendly with laws that give them an edge over more-established havens.

note — Havens do not attract foreign money by chance. They do it by design.

They intentionally restructured their laws to become more financially attractive. And they do it quite creatively.

As some havens are rising stars, others are losing their lustre. Switzerland was once considered the bastion for secret banking, but this is no longer true. Its ability to insure privacy has eroded, largely due to international (mostly United States) pressure. The same is true of the Bahamas and Caymans, who have recently attracted too much political attention. In turn, some of the smaller upstarts—the Cook Islands, Gibraltar, Nevis and the Turks—can guarantee more protection because they are less subject to international pressures.

Except for the old European stand-by havens—Switzerland, Liechtenstein, Austria and the Channel Islands—most havens are new to the game. And new ones continuously spring up. Gibraltar, for instance, only changed its laws in 1993 to become an attractive asset protection haven. Tiny St. Kitts in the Caribbean is now revamping its own laws to attract its share of international funds and compete with nearby havens—the Turks and Caicos, Antigua and the Caymans. Britain has spawned the greatest number of havens. England itself—while a key financial center in its own right—is not considered a haven chiefly because of its many treaties and close working relationships with the United States and other major countries. But it is a very different story with the British Flag Colonies—the Bahamas, Caymans, British Virgin Islands, Bermuda, Turks, Gibraltar and Malta. These colonies are sufficiently autonomous to enact their own tax and banking laws while considered economically and politically stable because of their British affiliation.

note

Whatever their size, history or geography, all havens share these distinguishing characteristics: laws and banking practices that help you escape taxes, protect your money from creditors, hide your wealth from prying eyes or build wealth faster than you can at home. While their goals are always similar, they vary considerably in how well they accomplish these different objectives.

Most offshore havens have an interesting history. We traditionally think first of Switzerland when we speak about offshore havens, but it was the Bank of England that deliberately rigged the Bahamas to become the world's first true haven, when in the early 1960s more money was leaving the Bahamas than arriving. To reverse this dismal trend, the Bahamas established the first two-tier tax and rigid banking laws to provide banking secrecy. Bahamians would pay higher taxes on their earned income while foreigners would enjoy a permanent tax holiday and tight financial secrecy. In the 40 years since, other countries in search of a *raison d'etre* also found that attracting capital from oppressed citizens elsewhere could be one profitable industry.

Not surprisingly, it was the long-overtaxed and financially exposed Americans who were first to seize this new opportunity and shift their enormous wealth to the waiting Bahamian banks. Beleaguered nationals from other financially oppressive countries were not far behind. The Bahamas soon had a flourishing new industry—international banking—and the race was on!

Poor countries continue to jump on the offshore bandwagon. Their ammunition? As always, laws to attract foreign investors: greater secrecy, stronger lawsuit protection, bigger tax benefits or more profitable investments. These remain the underpinnings on which offshore havens compete and attract money—and always will.

note Poor countries, particularly those without strong industry, still find that international banking can be their most profitable industry.

Offshore banking has grown enormously over the past 30 years. There are about 50 recognized havens scattered across the globe. (The more

HOT spot We know the tiny Caymans have more American dollars than do all the banks in Manhattan!

popular havens are profiled in the second section.) We will never know precisely how much American money is banked overseas because the havens' strict privacy laws keep such matters secret. But over $300 billion is thought to be in the Caribbean havens alone. The trend is accelerating. The number of offshore banks has nearly doubled in the past decade. However you measure it, offshore banking is the world's most explosive growth industry!

Offshore banking, as an industry, has also matured in many ways. The havens have become much more sophisticated—even ingenious—in how they compete for foreign money. They constantly rig new lending restrictions, investment limitations, reporting requirements, public disclosure laws on financial records or licensing of banking operations.

However they do it, eager, competitive offshore havens and flourishing offshore banks know what it takes to beckon investors from afar. Increasingly, these investors are foreign corporations. Offshore havens certainly have not escaped their attention. Major U.S. corporations busily devise their own clever ways to exploit the offshore opportunities.

For example, many American companies have their own offshore banking subsidiaries. Others tapped into the massive Eurodollar market to produce awesome profits. Still other savvy American corporations have learned how to exchange currency without restriction, shift investments, avoid taxes, gain financial privacy over competitors and snub their noses at the notoriously restrictive U.S. regulations. All this from simply stepping beyond our own borders! Offshore havens will continue to grow, prosper and attract money as

note The honeymoon continues between major American corporations and the offshore havens, which persistently grow, prosper and continue to attract even more foreign money.

long as they offer what Americans and other nationals so desperately want: freedom from confiscatory taxes, less red tape, unwarranted invasions of their privacy, more return on their investments and protection for their wealth. Can you benefit from this offshore banking explosion? If you have even modest wealth, then the answer is probably. If you have more wealth—or own a business—then the answer is absolutely!

Myth no. 1

Offshore banking is illegal

Why then do so many people cringe when you mention offshore havens? Because they foolishly believe the big lies and myths about offshore havens and offshore banking. The biggest myth, of course, is that it's illegal.

Undoubtedly, tax evaders, money-launderers and other scofflaws do take advantage of offshore haven's secrecy laws. But so do many legitimate, law-abiding citizens and corporations who are only taking legal advantage of another country's more enlightened laws without breaking the laws of their own country.

It's not necessary for one to go offshore to break a few laws since we have no shortage of tax evaders, money-launderers and other assorted criminals right here in the United States. A better case can be made that plenty of honest people bank offshore only because they can legally do there what would be illegal to do in the United States.

Americans who try to achieve these same financial objectives at home must resort to illegal activities to do so. If there is a crime, it is not on the part of those who bank elsewhere, but on the part of those who enact laws that make it necessary to bank elsewhere. They are the true robbers because it is they who rob you of your financial freedom!

Yes, it is easier to cheat the IRS by banking offshore. This puts overseas investors on the honor system. But if you dutifully report your offshore income to the IRS, your offshore bank account is as legal as banking on Main Street, U.S.A.

HOT spot Offshore banks do not report earned income to the IRS (although these offshore earnings are taxable).

Of course, Americans have not proven unimaginative in their ability to short-change the IRS—without their money leaving our shores. The size of our underground economy is staggering. And that's only the tip of the iceberg when you consider the many, many ways Americans, and most other nationals, have to cheat on their taxes. The point is that you need not go offshore to cheat on your taxes. And the fact that your money is offshore should draw no presumption that you do cheat. The illegality myth also springs from the common belief that Americans cannot legally take money out of the United States. But this too is incorrect. The fact is that the U.S. has never, does not now, and probably never will forbid Americans from investing their money overseas. Why?

note It is estimated that about one-third of our income goes unreported.

The United States depends too greatly upon international trade. Any law that prevents expatriation (removal from the country) of U.S. funds would hurt our balance of trade, and aggravate our growing trade deficit. America can't afford a policy that stops its citizens from worldwide banking and investing.

The U.S. does limit how much cash you can take out of the country without reporting it to the government. But, as you will see later, there are absolutely no restrictions on wiring funds or mailing checks to offshore banks or foreign companies. This is a freedom Americans should never forfeit through ignorance of our laws. To our credit, few countries let their citizens expatriate their funds as liberally as we do. But as a citizen or resident of the

United States, you may, with few minor exceptions, legally keep your money anywhere in the world without restriction on amount.

And how can offshore banking be considered illicit when you survey the many major corporations who actively bank offshore? Exxon, Sears, Firestone, Boeing and Rockwell International are some of the more notable on a very long list of well-known names from the ranks of corporate America. Most of America's

> *note* While corporate America has long taken advantage of the global money markets, individual investors have only more recently caught the fever.

wealthy families, and a litany of political leaders, athletes, movie stars and other highly visible people, maintain foreign bank accounts or offshore trusts to protect and build their wealth.

The American banking industry—working closely with the IRS to propagandize against offshore banking—would be the last to let you know that it fervently supports offshore banking. After all, plenty of money from American bankers is offshore. U.S. banks with overseas branches include Chase Manhattan, Citibank, First National Bank, Bank of America and hundreds of others.

What is amazing is that in these enlightened times, most Americans are

> *note* The U.S. government, and our banking industry, will continue their organized propaganda campaign. They will forever paint offshore havens as illegal and criminal.

still hoodwinked into believing that offshore havens are only illicit criminal hideaways. Unfortunately, most Americans have not checked out the facts—and won't—because they don't know how they can benefit from offshore banking. This is unfortunate, because most people can benefit from offshore banking in so many different ways.

To the extent the lies and distortions of the U.S. government and our banking industry succeed, Americans will keep their money here in the United States where it can be easily controlled, taxed and exploited. You should not be victimized by this propaganda campaign. If you choose to do so, you can reclaim your financial freedom and do so legally by moving all your wealth offshore.

Myth no. 2

Offshore banking is too complicated, costly, confusing

Granted, in the early days, offshore banking was much more complicated. But the world is shrinking. New technology now allows you to bank overseas as easily and conveniently as you can bank down the street. To open an offshore account, you simply write to an offshore bank for the necessary forms along with its instructions. Withdrawing money from your offshore account is just as simple because you can write a check or draft against your offshore account for deposit into your U.S. bank account. The transfer can be completed in a few days or even instantly with wire or electronic transfers. What can be faster or simpler?

Yes, you can now be an international investor from the comfort of your own home or office. All you need is a pen and a telephone. The few quirks of offshore banking can be learned overnight. And language is not a problem since most havens transact business in English. So do their lawyers, accountants and other professionals who aid international

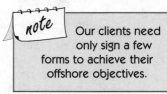

note Our clients need only sign a few forms to achieve their offshore objectives.

investors banking or conduct business within the haven. Moreover, most—if not all—of the offshore arrangements can be handled by American firms, such as my own Garrett Group, which specialize in offshore banking and international asset protection plans.

Even if you should prefer to travel to your offshore haven, you can probably do so quite conveniently. Most of the popular havens used by Americans are within two to three hours flight time from the eastern United States and have regular air service from most major airports. Offshore banking is not very costly. It may cost several hundred to several thousand dollars to set up a foreign company or asset protection trusts to protect your assets or save you taxes, but this is not a cost. It is a very good investment. Spending a few thousand dollars now can save you millions later. Moreover, it is no more costly to set up companies and trusts offshore than right here in America.

note The expense of a few long-distance faxes and phone calls is negligible.

And standard offshore bank accounts are no more difficult or costly to open than American bank accounts. You will find that it is more costly to do business in some havens than others, and this certainly should be a factor when choosing a haven. Your professional advisor can give you a reasonably accurate estimate of costs for the various services you may require.

As an offshore investor you won't be swamped with tons of extra paperwork. Offshore havens usually impose no taxes on non-residents, so they require no tax returns. And to report your offshore earnings to the IRS, you need only complete a few additional items on your standard tax return. Offshore banking may sound complicated and confusing and that is part of their mystique. But in reality international banking is remarkably easy, efficient and inexpensive. Don't let anybody tell you differently.

Myth no. 3

Offshore banking is too risky

Whoever lulled us into the myth that only U.S. banks are safe? Because U.S. bank accounts (under $100,000) are insured by the FDIC, we believe banks elsewhere are less safe.

> ⚠️ **CAUTION**
> A severe run on the banks will quickly deplete the FDIC reserves, and, if we are hit with another serious depression, who can guarantee that Uncle Sam will dip into the general treasury to back up its FDIC obligations?

The sorry fact is that it is our FDIC-insured accounts that are least safe. Our government has precious few dollars available to back up the trillions of dollars on deposit. Once uncommon in the United States, bank failures have become too common. In 1980, the FDIC reported only 200 problem banks. By 1988 the number rose to over 1,500. A problem bank is one whose fiscal health has deteriorated to the point it is no longer stable. The level of profits for non-failing, non-problem banks has also deteriorated sharply since 1982. American banks now operate at their worst performance level since the depression. Our entire banking system is but an economic blip away from disaster.

The plain truth is that American bankers have become poor guardians of their depositors' money.

The question should not be: why should an American trust a bank offshore? The more informed would ask: why would anyone want an American bank account?

HOT spot That they are not FDIC insured is a selling point for offshore banks! If they were FDIC insured, they would also be FDIC regulated and subject to the same bureaucratic and protectionist banking regulations as other FDIC banks. Surprisingly, some offshore banks are FDIC regulated, but fortunately not many. In fact, it is because American banks are FDIC insured that they have become sloppy with their money. This allows our U.S. banks to make the risky loans that have brought about the great savings and loan debacle that will cost American taxpayers over $500 billion to straighten out. Nothing

> 📝 **note**
> Depositors do not choose their banks on their financial strength because they instead rely on the FDIC.

comparable has been seen in any foreign country where bankers are held accountable to their depositors.

note

Because offshore banks are seldom under the yoke of the FDIC, that doesn't mean they are unregulated. Every country has banking laws and rules. Many havens feature a depositor insurance program similar to our FDIC, but with far fewer restrictions. Independent insurance companies—rather than a government agency—usually insure 100 percent of an offshore depositors' funds, not merely $100,000 as is insured by the FDIC. For that reason, offshore havens are safer for the larger depositor.

HOT spot Offshore rules are less restrictive than U.S. banking laws, so offshore banks operate with greater flexibility, earn much more money for their investors and pay higher interest to their depositors than the overregulated U.S. banks.

Almost all offshore banks are self-insured, which means they must have 100 percent liquidity. Every $1 on deposit must be backed by $1 in liquid assets. In contrast, FDIC insured U.S. banks maintain a liquidity equal to about 10 percent of their deposits.

Here's a real eye-opener: Not one of the largest, strongest or most profitable banks in the world is in the United States. But this should hardly be surprising. Remember, no other country has ever had as many bank failures as we did under the S&L scandal. Offshore banks very seldom fail.

How to find that right bank will be covered in depth in Chapter 7. And the cautious investor will shop carefully for that right bank. Fortunately, there are a number of ways to identify the long-established and highly solvent offshore banks. Prudent investors also diversify and spread their money among several banks and even different havens. This virtually eliminates any risk associated with offshore banking.

E-Z TIP By all statistics, offshore banking is considerably safer than banking here in the U.S.—if you choose the right bank.

Myth no. 4

Offshore banking is only for the wealthy

Unfortunately, most Americans are taxed so heavily that they can't scrape together enough money to build a respectable savings account here in the United States. But even the poor must shed still another myth—that offshore banking is only for the super-rich. You can open an offshore account with as little as $100. It is practical to do so if you have $50,000 to bank. It is foolish not to when you have $100,000 or more to invest offshore! Many Americans with modest wealth are mortgaging their assets to keep them safe from predators at home—litigants, the IRS, ex-spouses—who can quickly devastate their wealth. The mortgage proceeds are safely banked offshore and earn more than enough interest to pay the mortgage.

HOT spot Remember this point I made earlier: you need not belong to the monied class to benefit from offshore banking.

But even small depositors can increase their yield by 50 percent or more by banking offshore. That added income can be important to the middle-class American struggling to get by. It can be critical to America's elderly who must survive on a fixed income which is in turn threatened by a shaky Social Security system.

Of course, no self-respecting offshore bank will subject itself to our restrictions because it would then lose the flexibility that gives the offshore bank its competitive edge.

note Americans know very little about offshore banks, or their very attractive interest rates, because offshore banks are restricted by law from advertising within the U.S. unless they agree to be regulated like American banks.

Offshore banks pay higher interest than American banks for two big reasons. First, American banks have their interest rates regulated by law. Uncle Sam determines what a bank pays in interest, even if the bank can afford higher rates. Offshore banks, on the other hand, as true free-market operations, function without governmental controls on the interest they charge or pay. Offshore banks characteristically also operate with greater efficiency and lower overhead than do American banks. They learned how to operate without the fancy building and costly frills that eat into what American bankers could otherwise pay to their depositors.

note

Over the past year, I have helped many clients open offshore accounts in the Bahamas, Caymans, Cook Islands, Turks, Isle of Man, Switzerland and other sound havens. These were not wealthy people. They were plumbers, consultants, accountants, pharmacists, small business owners and other mainstream middle-class Americans. They typify the flood of Americans who go offshore to avoid further erosion of their limited wealth in U.S. banks. Their offshore bank accounts average under $100,000. No, you need not be a Rockefeller to enjoy the offshore experience.

Logic and reason please!

From all this you can see that offshore banking is, in itself, neither evil, immoral, illegal or unethical. You have every right to put your money offshore and every reason to do so—as you will further see in the next chapter. Yet you probably never thought too much about foreign or offshore banking.

You will soon see how offshore banking can give you higher investment profits, lower taxes, more financial safety and wealth protection, and a new sense of privacy and security.

Your first step is to shed those fuzzy ideas and prejudices against offshore banking. Keep an open mind. Investigate the real facts. It is indeed a big world out there with truly great places to put your money!

Key points to remember

◆ Contrary to popular myth, you don't have to be a millionaire or criminal to benefit from offshore banking.

◆ Offshore banks are appreciably safer than American banks—and pay higher interest. The fact is that offshore banking is less risky than banking at home.

◆ You can quickly and conveniently do all your offshore banking using nothing more than a telephone or a fax machine.

◆ The expense associated with offshore banking is usually modest—and invariably worth the benefits offered.

The offshore megatrend

2

Chapter 2

The offshore megatrend

If you were to meet and talk to the millions of Americans who happily bank, invest or do business offshore, you would hear a wide variety of explanations of why their money is overseas. Some reasons are legal, others illegal.

Most objectives are logical, but you'll also hear foolish, unsound or unattainable schemes. Regardless of the reason, the trend continues. Why do people send their money offshore? Why should you put your money offshore?

Whatever their reasons, or yours, the evidence is mounting that many more Americans, as well as swarms of financially oppressed nationals from other major industrialized countries, are seeking their financial freedom in offshore havens.

Those who bank, invest or conduct business offshore usually try to satisfy one particular financial need or objective.

> **note**
>
> Reasons for offshore investing may be financial privacy, relief from oppressive taxes, protection from lawsuits and creditors, a more relaxed regulatory climate, or less governmental intrusion.

Regardless of the objective, whether it is an individual investor with modest wealth, a major corporation or bank—each has its money offshore because it is the only way they can gain the financial freedom they want!

Those who invest and do business internationally become "free world" citizens (or "international men", as described by best-selling investment author Doug Casey) because they discovered that through offshore havens they could avoid taxation, transaction-reporting, investment restrictions, burdensome bureaucratic red tape and mountains of unfair and unworkable laws that increasingly strip us of the financial freedoms we once enjoyed here in America. In essence, when you become that offshore investor you become "government-proof." You substitute your country's onerous laws for friendlier laws found elsewhere.

Doug Casey's description of the offshore investor, *as one running from Big Brother*, only tells half the story. To be sure, many Americans bank overseas to lessen their tax bite or do business in a less bureaucratic climate. This will always be true. Yet many more Americans are going offshore for a variety of other reasons. This chapter highlights some of these reasons. The chapters that follow will explore each of these offshore opportunities in much greater depth.

The offshore exodus

Offshore havens are big business. Mighty big business! Because money moves offshore very quietly, we lack solid statistics to demonstrate exactly how big the offshore industry has become. But scattered data allows us to speculate. For instance, we know non-resident Caribbean bank deposits are over one trillion dollars—compared to a paltry two billion in 1980. You must

> **note**
>
> It is not unreasonable to assume offshore investments are between three to four trillion dollars. That's a lot of money!

keep in mind that this growth was despite the fact that many newer and even more competitive havens also compete for foreign investment. To put it in perspective, the offshore industry is about four times what we spend for health care in the United States each year. It's also growing at a far faster rate as our economy becomes more global. Americans are suddenly waking up to the many opportunities abroad. About one in four Americans who earn over $100,000 a year now invests offshore. The steady stream of planes and cruise ships from mainland U.S.A. to such places as the Bahamas, Caymans, the British Virgin Islands and other exotic spots ferry more than work-weary, vacationing Americans. They are packed with Americans who are visiting their money!

You can't miss this growing interest in offshore havens. A seminar on offshore haven investing would draw scant attendance only a decade ago. Today they bring sell-out crowds. Books on the topic are grabbed up as soon as they tumble from the printing press. Americans are developing an insatiable appetite to learn whatever they can about offshore investing. More accurately, it is an insatiable appetite for renewed financial freedom. As pointed out in Chapter 1, while offshore banking has always been legal, it is only now gaining respectability. This new-found respectability further fuels the trend. It is not so much the vast numbers of Americans who are offshore with their money as the respectability of those who are leading the parade.

> **STRATEGY**
>
> Americans only now are awakening to the fact that going offshore with their money is their only way to achieve this financial freedom as taxes climb and economic restrictions tighten.

Who's who offshore? Who leads this exodus to more promised lands? Some of the best names in American industry: Sears, Boeing, Continental Oil, Exxon, Monsanto, Firestone and hundreds of other fortune 1000 firms.

Joining this offshore parade are the premier banks: Chase Manhattan, Citibank, Security Pacific, Bank of America and hundreds of other blue-chip banks who know offshore banking is a savvy if not essential financial strategy, although they will never admit it to you! You can even find the veritable American Express in the Caymans, Hong Kong and nearly every other important haven.

These institutions aren't merely dabbling offshore. They're in neck deep. They have much of their portfolios offshore and their offshore activities generate the lion's share of their profits.

Still, offshore havens are not the exclusive playground for the rich and famous. Smaller businesses find equal opportunities offshore. Maybe even more opportunity. They start small banks, leasing companies, import-export, manufacturing and countless other firms whose growth would be stymied at home.

The offshore exodus grows daily. And this offshore trend is nowhere near its peak. Right now you, as an American, can legally put your money offshore. But historically governments have reacted strongly when too much of their resident savings are sent to foreign banks. Not only are funds drained from the local economy, but the drain exerts a downward pressure on their currency on the international exchange markets.

note

The offshore movement will only accelerate in the years ahead as the search for financial freedom becomes even more urgent.

When will Americans join most of the other countries who prevent their residents from taking their money out of the country? It's hard to say. But that day may come. That is why you must act before it is too late!

Why you must put your money offshore

For what compelling reasons should you go offshore with your money? The answer is that offshore havens can help you achieve your own brand of financial freedom in a variety of ways, but nine big reasons prod most people to move their money offshore:

Financial privacy

Perhaps you don't mind governmental snoops and other prying eyes probing your financial affairs. I do. So do countless other Americans. That's why they put their wealth offshore where strict offshore secrecy laws vigorously shield their banking and other financial records from the eyes of the IRS, creditors, competitors, ex-spouses and others with a keen—if unwarranted—interest in their wealth.

HOT spot Only offshore havens can keep your affairs truly private, unlike here in the United States where your life and financial affairs are an open book.

You can never appreciate the offshore secrecy advantage until you have suffered the indignity of someone snooping through your financial and private affairs—which is so easily accomplished here in the United States.

In subsequent chapters, you will see that it is both possible and legal to remain absolutely invisible offshore because most offshore havens have laws that rigorously protect financial secrecy and confidentiality. In fact, disclosure of a depositor's banking and other confidential financial information in most havens is illegal and punishable by severe fines or even imprisonment.

E-Z TIP Offshore havens don't give lip service to confidentiality. They mean it!

Who needs financial secrecy? You do! Whether your reasons are business, personal, fiscal or even political. You may want to hide your money from your ex-spouse chasing alimony, hide financial information from heirs, or simply feel that your finances are nobody's business but your own. Or you may be convinced that financial privacy discourages con artists, kidnappers and thieves. These are a few of the reasons people gravitate to havens where privacy and secrecy are considered the foundation of personal liberty and financial freedom.

note Offshore havens have a confidentiality standard that perfectly meets the need for secrecy in the marketplace.

Secrecy is no less important to businesses that want to protect sensitive financial and proprietary information from competitors, suppliers, customers or the government. This sensitive proprietary information may be the business's principal asset. Or a company may want to keep certain financial information from the IRS, potential litigants, employees, and even prospective buyers.

Tax protection

Americans mostly associate offshore havens with tax avoidance or evasion. Offshore havens have at least partly earned a reputation as tax havens because they can help you legitimately escape domestic taxes through offshore financial arrangements. Others are not legal. Many offshore tax schemes are questionable and operate in a "gray zone." Unfortunately, the best offshore tax loopholes have been narrowed in more recent years because our friends at the IRS continuously and enthusiastically attempt to completely close both legitimate and illegitimate opportunities to escape our confiscatory U.S. income and estate taxes.

note In most major countries, tax evasion is an accepted way of life—even a sport. We have a different culture. Most Americans are comparatively honest with their taxes. This may less express our patriotism than our deep-seated fear of the IRS. But clear signs abound that many more Americans are becoming tax scofflaws and cheats. The underground economy is swelling. And it is understandable. Inflation has moved more Americans into higher tax brackets. Our tax rates constantly increase to cover our mounting federal deficits. Middle-class Americans are tired of supporting welfare recipients, financing mammoth social welfare programs and aiding other countries. They now see taxes as inequitable and excessive. And because the IRS must now chase many more errant taxpayers, the tax evaders believe they have a better chance of beating the tax man—whether their derelictions are at home or abroad.

CAUTION

It would be naive and insulting to your intelligence to suggest people don't use offshore havens to illegally beat the tax collector. Many do. Championing that objective, however, is not my purpose. Nor is it a matter of morality or honesty. I just don't think it's smart for Americans to break the law when they can easily take advantage of the many legal ways to avoid or reduce taxes through offshore banking using the tax-saving strategies I reveal in Chapter 6. You will then see why I and many others call offshore havens the "Ultimate Tax Shelter."

A wonderful feature of the offshore haven is that it lets you combine tax savings with one or more other benefits—such as asset protection, privacy or global investing. Whether tax savings is your primary objective or a secondary goal, it is always a powerful inducement for the offshore investor.

> **E-Z TIP**
> Even if you cannot completely eliminate taxes by banking offshore, you're bound to find many ways to reduce or defer your taxes.

Asset protection

Asset protection is my professional specialty, so I have a growing stream of clients seeking refuge in offshore havens. They want to shield their wealth from lawsuits, the IRS, creditors, ex-spouses and others who can put their assets in danger. Obviously, there is no shortage of people who need asset protection.

Offshore havens can offer iron-clad asset protection. Sheltering your wealth in one or more of these havens may be the only way to successfully protect it from attack. Offshore asset protection provides considerably more protection than do conventional domestic asset protection strategies—such as titling assets in irrevocable

CAUTION Assets retitled and left within the United States may be successfully set aside as fraudulent transfers. There is virtually no need to fear this when your assets are offshore.

trusts, family limited partnerships or even relying upon the state exemptions.

Perhaps you haven't noticed, but there is a lawsuit epidemic in America. And you can as easily get into serious trouble with the IRS or an ex-spouse. Building your own personal financial fortress offshore is your best way to keep your money in your pocket!

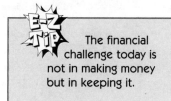

E-Z TIP The financial challenge today is not in making money but in keeping it.

You can keep your wealth 100 percent safe, but, only if you know the haven to choose for your financial fortress and how to build the strongest fortress.

Smart Americans no longer wait until they get into financial trouble before they protect their money. They go offshore today for fear of what may happen tomorrow. While offshore havens may be your only safe path for a last-minute escape from creditors, well-heeled, vulnerable people defensively position their wealth in safe havens before trouble strikes. Defensive financial planning is absolutely necessary in these perilous times and will become more so in the years ahead.

Diversification

Whether by company or industry, smart investors diversify to spread their risk. Smart investors also diversify geographically. They never put all their investment eggs in one basket.

With global diversification, you never bet your entire nest egg on the economic or political stability of any one country. Like all smart investors, you too must spread your nest egg globally. Why this advice?

Consider Germany. In the 1930's, Germany had unprecedented runaway inflation. German marks became nearly worthless. In the 1940's German Jews and other persecuted minorities couldn't get their wealth out of the country. We witnessed comparable events in Russia, Cuba and countless banana republics. Latin Americans and Western Europeans routinely forfeit their wealth through confiscation or economic erosion. Who is to say it can't happen here?

 If you believe offshore banking is too risky, the statistics will show that you significantly reduce your investment risk when you invest globally— rather than limit yourself to U.S. investments. That is what's risky!

As you will see in Chapter 3, international diversification cuts risk and improves investment performance. In a worst case scenario, a combination of foreign exchange losses and high inflation can quickly wipe out savings. Yet, this has been the case in recent years for those who hold their savings in dollars—as Americans with mainland savings have found out.

> *note* The decline in the dollar exchange rate and the dwindling American influence on international commerce are only two good reasons to invest overseas.

It has always been legal for Americans to take their money out of the country (subject only to certain reporting requirements). But someday you may not be able to. This will happen when too many Americans lose confidence in our economy and too much "flight-capital" leaves the country. Then, as happened in so many other cases, the government will clamp the lid on the flight-capital. Then it will be too late to enjoy the financial safety and prosperity that only comes when your money is spread among a number of nations. When your wealth rides the waves of a global economy, you are no longer vulnerable to one nation's economy.

Higher interest rates

Not too long ago American banks paid depositors about 12 percent interest. There was then little reason to seek higher interest rates elsewhere. That was then. American banks now pay one-third that rate while offshore banks still routinely pay their depositors twice that interest. Nor are these offshore banks wobbly or high-risk. They are healthy, long-established financial institutions that are as stable as any American bank.

A sizeable chunk of American investment capital is in foreign securities, but even more is deposited in offshore banks. Beyond tax, privacy and asset protection, it is the offshore banks' attractive interest rates that chiefly draw American money. These rates match the returns available at home only with higher-risk securities.

Why is this so? Because in the United States, bank interest is largely regulated by the federal government, so American banks can't always keep pace with the unregulated offshore banks.

> *note*
> Offshore banks also operate with lower overhead and greater efficiency. They can afford to pay their depositors more.

The net consequence is that billions of American dollars are no longer in American banks but in Bahamian, Cayman, Austrian or Swiss banks. Almost any place you throw a dart on the world map are banks that pay higher interest than their American counterparts.

> **E-Z TIP** With high-tech electronic banking, Americans are finding that they can as easily bank in Hong Kong, Singapore or Austria as in a local bank. They also find the offshore bank usually pays bigger dividends.

American bankers are lucky that relatively few Americans realize how much more they could earn on their money overseas. Unfortunately, most Americans will never know because our protectionist federal laws prevent offshore banks from advertising in the United States. But Americans now travel and read more and are becoming more enlightened!

This explains why countless retirees and other fixed-income Americans who are forced to live on their savings, consider our low interest rates a slow route to starvation and increasingly go to the far shore for the income they need. The rest of us are not far behind.

Profit opportunities

As you will see in subsequent chapters, aside from higher interest, offshore havens are also burgeoning with other great investment opportunities. Global investing has become an exciting and rewarding experience !

One example is offshore securities and mutual funds. When purchased through a tax haven trust they are less costly, more flexible and consistently more profitable than comparable U.S. investments. Many more Americans also now trade in Eurodollars and other foreign currencies that also have proven stronger than the American dollar on the international exchanges.

Additionally, foreign investments offer important features unknown to domestic investments. Asset protection and privacy, for example, is yours when you buy Swiss annuities.

As I say, exciting things are happening in the international investment arena—and much of it is happening elsewhere outside the United States.

Passive investment abroad is only one part of the story. Many more American financiers and entrepreneurs now freely roam the globe in search of super-profitable business deals. Their travels are now as likely to lead them to tiny Caribbean, Pacific rim or emerging third-world havens as to London, Tokyo or other leading financial centers. The trend continues, so Wall Street must beware. As savvy investors and aggressive business people increasingly migrate to offshore markets, this new breed of international investor and entrepreneur will obliterate the notion that business must be done within our own borders. The globe is now everybody's new playing field.

Protection from economic chaos

Another reason to diversify offshore is to seek refuge from economic chaos when you fear economic ruin at home. Many Americans do believe an economic apocalypse will soon be upon us and that it will devastate America financially.

I disagree with the apocalypse theory. Still, doomsday predictions have some basis when you consider that the United States' deficit is astronomical and growing daily. Sadly, we are now a debtor nation, and one unable to pay its debts. Foreign investors who enthusiastically acquired American investments now invest elsewhere where even better investment opportunities can be found.

> *note* Americans, equally jittery about our financial stability, also seek their economic stability abroad.

When will our open door policy that allows mass movements of cash or "flight capital" to more economically stable offshore havens cause Washington to close the doors? As I say, only time will tell. But until then, the many who see a deteriorating America and believe economic safety lies beyond our shores bring a compelling message home for the rest of us.

Friendly business environment

America was once the citadel of free enterprise and a great place to be in business.

That was then. Things are far different now. The fun is gone. The unhappy fact is that nowadays it is too difficult, too costly and too much of a hassle to do business in America.

Business regulation swelled enormously since World War II, yet the exodus of American businesses to less bureaucratic countries is relatively new. On the other hand, multinational companies that can operate from within any country seldom select America and its strangle-hold laws. We

HOT spot People in every industry and profession are literally drowning in a sea of oppressive governmental regulation and bureaucratic red tape.

are also losing ground to more far-sighted havens that have learned how to attract businesses with enticing relocation incentives, low taxes and a hands-off policy from their government. This trend toward offshore business started in the 1970's, grew quickly in the 1980's with the emergence of the Eurocurrency markets, and continues today at an even faster pace.

U.S. companies bemoan our slow-moving bureaucratic system, claiming it prevents them from operating as efficiently or as profitably as they could elsewhere. More than a few are doing something about it. So we see them forming captive insurance companies outside the U.S. to circumvent our archaic insurance regulations. We see mutual funds chartered offshore to avoid our anachronistic SEC and IRS requirements. We even see it in education with offshore medical schools that compete against the "protectionist" American medical establishment. And we even see it with offshore gambling. Countries a few scant miles offshore, such as the Bahamas, profitably conduct even that industry with less burdensome, costly and restrictive gaming licenses compared to those of Atlantic City or Las Vegas.

note Granted, not every mom and pop business can pack up and move overseas, but swarms of businesses from overly regulated industries can and do. The trend will escalate.

More importantly, we now see more offshore research and development. Our restrictions for developing drugs, toxic substances and munitions force the less patient researchers overseas. Companies that want to exploit their inventions are not far behind.

It's not always a matter of over-regulation. Offshore havens are simply more user-friendly to businesses. For instance, it is comparatively easy to set up an offshore bank and reap windfall benefits that would be impossible through U.S. bank ownership.

HINT The greater ability to raise capital offshore is for many business owners a big plus for going offshore, where they have easier access to the deposit-laden offshore banks which lend more aggressively, creatively and willingly than do more conservative and over-regulated American banks.

Offshore havens become particularly attractive to offshore companies who set up their own offshore banks. Owning their own bank, they can creatively and effectively invest in foreign currency markets, loan money to themselves, reduce currency controls, arrange for parallel loans and engage in a wide variety of financial gymnastics they could never achieve at home.

STRATEGY Combining the benefits of offshore banking with escaping the American stranglehold of regulation is a powerful magnet to all progressive companies who seek greater profit, privacy and freedom from bureaucratic controls.

This self-sponsored offshore banking also makes it much easier for these businesses to engage in international trade, where for instance, the offshore bank can issue to the company letters of credit or third-party guarantees on outside loans.

Personal factors

Americans are not always in offshore havens for financial reasons alone. Some are drawn to the offshore haven's comfortable, low-cost lifestyle, particularly retirees who can no longer live comfortably here on Social Security but can live like royalty in places like the Bahamas, Mexico or Ireland.

For others, offshore havens present excellent employment opportunities, and even the possibility to escape U.S. taxes on those earnings. With an

The case for global investing

3

Chapter 3

The case for global investing

I urge my clients to at least partly invest offshore. Inevitably, they ask why they should invest outside the United States when we have the best investments right here in America. The answer is that there are too many exciting things happening elsewhere in the world—new and innovative investment opportunities that are unmatched here at home. That's why offshore investments now attract more American capital than do U.S. investments!

While America has done little to modernize its investment structure, other countries have passed laws to encourage new and creative financial products. Investments such as the Swiss Plus and Gold Plan are two highly popular investments you will learn more about later in this chapter.

America is also no longer the bastion of big business. Many of the world's fastest growing companies are not headquartered here but elsewhere.

55

Coca-Cola, Ford, Boeing and other household names are not exclusively American companies, but instead are multinational companies.

Frigidaire, Travelodge, Purina Dog Chow, Baskin Robbins—do you still think of these as American products? Hardly. These and hundreds of other "American" brands are now overseas imports. Check out the world's top 1,000 companies. You will see the vitality of overseas industry and why international stocks consistently outperform U.S. stocks. You will find the fast-growing international capital market particularly attractive if you are a fixed-income investor. More money is now invested in worldwide bonds than worldwide equities. Offshore bonds account for over half of the total bond market.

note

The investment world will soon be a world without boundaries. The global investment market will soon be upon us. By pressing a computer button you will be able to buy shares on the New York Stock Exchange in a Mexican or German factory. As trillions of dollars, or equivalent currency, flows freely across the borders, the market will become even more efficient. There will be many new investment instruments. Traders and fund managers—not politicians and bankers—will influence this global investment market. New technologies will make possible the necessary information flow.

All this will happen. But it hasn't happened yet. For now, we must go beyond our own borders to tap the global investment opportunities.

This does not mean you can't find good investments right here in the United States. We have our share of good financial deals. If one economy slumps, another is bound to rise. American investors can no longer bet all their chips on the U.S. economy. They must hedge their bets through global investing.

HOT spot The big reason to go offshore, with at least part of your wealth, is to achieve the safety and stability that only comes through diversification.

And as I say in other chapters, it's sensible to deploy some of your assets offshore for reasons other than making money. It's also the best way to keep it from the greedy reach of government, lawsuit-crazy litigants or other parasites who want your money in their pockets. Many American investors hesitate to invest outside the U.S. because they are comfortable with American investment practices and customs. You may also hesitate. You know who you are dealing with here. Your money is nearby. You are familiar with things.

At one time this would be sufficient reason to ignore the foreign markets. That is no longer true. Today there are simply too many compelling reasons to invest offshore. No knowledgeable, serious investor can believe otherwise.

> **note**
> Yes, global investing will require you to deal with entirely new politics, economics, laws, customs and even languages. But this is an exciting part of the game because it adds new dimensions to your investments when you broaden the playing field.

Americans are discovering that the offshore investment rules create a much more level playing field than they have at home. Foreign countries know how to woo the American dollar while our own politicians understand only how to take more of our money, stifle industry, competition and investment markets, and create confiscatory taxes to rob the wealth of those with money. That's why American wealth now heads for friendlier lands.

Do I foresee a coming apocalypse for America? Of course not. America is still a wonderful land and a world economic leader. But America is hurting—even if it is not quite down for the count. You, too, should believe America has a strong future and believe it will soon stage a comeback. But you must face two facts:

1) The American economy is wobbly

2) If your wealth is invested entirely in our economy, and our economy continues its plunge, then your standard of living must fall dramatically.

HOT spot

On the other hand, as an international profiteer, your door opens to spectacular investments and profit-making opportunities unknown with American investments. Only when you dabble in the offshore marketplace can you:

- Reap spectacular offshore interest rates, often 10 to 40 percent above what our U.S. banks pay. And your money is as safe in offshore banks, if not safer, as it is in our American banks that collapse with disturbing regularity.

- Invest in top-rated foreign investments that grow two, three or even four times as fast as comparable U.S. investments.

- Exploit the burgeoning overseas stock markets whose gains routinely double or triple the Dow Jones.

- Capitalize on a cornucopia of new, exciting and innovative offshore financial products that are unknown here at home.

- Experience the buoyancy that comes from dealing in rising—not declining—economies.

These and other opportunities are to be found beyond our shores. And these global investment opportunities are no more risky than the more sluggish American investments with considerably less potential. What is risky today is to gamble your wealth on one country—particularly when that country lags so badly behind in the international race. Take a lesson from the international profiteers who understand this need to diversify.

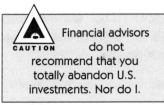

Financial advisors do not recommend that you totally abandon U.S. investments. Nor do I.

Financial advisers once counseled their American clients to invest no more than 10 or 20 percent of their money offshore. These same advisers now suggest 50 to 70 percent should be invested in foreign markets. We only recommend more of a portfolio shift toward offshore opportunities.

You may think global investing only lets you earn more from your investments. That's only partly true. Foreign stocks generally have outgrown U.S. stocks. If you had invested 50 percent of your money in foreign stocks over the past 25 years, your portfolio today would be worth about 15 percent more than if you were totally invested in American stocks. Had you invested overseas exclusively you would now be about 30 percent richer.

HOT spot Foreign securities are less volatile than U.S. securities. That's their big plus!

Still, I think the stronger argument for global investing is to reduce your investment risk. American stocks also are overpriced compared to foreign stocks. There are many ways to compare performance between foreign and U.S. stocks, but the best method is to compare the "price-to-book," or a company's book value against the price of its shares.

With that yardstick, American stocks lose hands down. U.S. stocks in the Standard and Poor's 500 sell at roughly two and a half times their book value. Foreign market securities sell for about twice their book value. You get a bigger bang for your buck with offshore stocks. The evidence that makes the case for offshore investing is overwhelming. These are only a few examples among many more. So what stops you from becoming that profiteer?

As an American, no law prohibits you from investing in foreign bonds or overseas corporations. It is not a crime to open a secret offshore bank account. If you consider the spectacular performance of many foreign investments, you

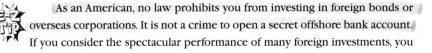

must agree it would be foolish not to dabble offshore. But don't be too quick to throw your wealth into offshore investments. Diversify slowly. Understand the foreign markets so you can invest intelligently.

To start modestly, invest a few dollars in an international mutual fund or buy shares in several leading overseas corporations. Or open a small savings account in one or more havens that I profile in this book. This is how you take your first baby step into the world of international profiteering.

But do start your journey as an international profiteer today. Reap the benefits of other economies. As a global investor you become a citizen of the world. That is what you must do to financially survive today and prosper tomorrow.

Avoid the dollar dip

Have you noticed that the dollar is sagging? Financially savvy Americans realize the only way to avoid the wealth-robbing effect of the falling dollar is to trade in foreign currencies, bonds, stocks and other investments that are stronger than the dollar. Once you move your money into strong overseas currencies, you will also see how seriously the dollar is fluctuating in value. As your foreign currency investments increase in value against the dollar, you can then convert them into even more dollars to spend or invest at home. Any change in the dollar's value automatically revalues your foreign-based investments. International stock or bond funds, for example, see their net asset values rise faster when the dollar's value declines because those investments then rise in real value when compared to the dollar.

Look back. You will see many periods of severe dollar devaluation. Even when our stock market boomed—as in the 1960's and again in the 1980's—it was outperformed significantly by foreign mutual funds.

The saga of the eroding dollar is painful. It is far less painful when you intelligently diversify your investments to ride the rise in foreign currencies. But to gain that hedge, you must invest in foreign currencies, not U.S. dollars.

You can accomplish this easily, whether you buy your foreign currency investments here or overseas. Money in Swiss banks, for example, is always in Swiss francs. British bonds pay interest in British pounds. Japanese mutual funds are valued in yen, whether purchased in Tokyo, New York or San Francisco.

> HINT
>
> The big challenge is to pick those currencies that are most likely to perform best in the future and remain strong against the dollar.

There are about 200 currencies globally. Obviously, not all outperform the dollar. Many only matched or even fell against the dollar over the past two decades. But 15 or more currencies did appreciate at least 25 percent over the American dollar. The most compelling argument for international investing can be made by comparing the appreciation of these 15 currencies.

Currency against the dollar (1970-1990)

1) Swiss franc 245%
2.) Japanese yen 182%
3) West German mark 150%
4) Austrian schilling 150%
5) Dutch guilder 120%
6) Singapore dollar 75%
7) Luxembourg franc 58%
8) Belgian franc 57%
9) Taiwanese dollar 50%
10) Maltese liva 40%
11) Rwandan franc 33%
12) Gatar riyal 31%
13) United Arab Emirates dirham 30%
14) Libyan dinar 27%
15) Bahrain dinar 26%

The lesson here is two-fold: First, America is hardly scraping bottom in terms of currency collapse. Ninety-five foreign currencies lost value against the dollar since 1970. Two-thirds dipped by more than 50 percent. You can lose as well as profit with offshore currencies. The key is to trade the right currencies. To know the secret can be your passport to a fortune!

How do you pick winning currencies? There is no easy answer. But don't assume the industrialized or militarily powerful countries are automatically your best bet. Look instead for countries with historically stable currencies and constant currency growth. Four recommendations:

1) The Swiss franc

The Swiss franc has been remarkably stable for more than a century. Since 1970, the Swiss franc skyrocketed over 250 percent against the dollar. It also remained strong against the gold and silver standards—always an important fiscal barometer.

Why does the Swiss currency perform so well? It is not Switzerland's strong industry, but Switzerland's leadership as a world financial center, and the great economic and social stability this tiny nation represents. Switzerland's political structure also contributes. Switzerland's unique sense of community makes politics a grass roots affair and creates a decentralization that keeps Switzerland politically vibrant. This is what imparts unification and economic stability to this formidable financial center. I expect the Swiss franc to appreciate less spectacularly in the forthcoming years, but the franc will unquestionably stay an excellent investment.

Buying Swiss annuities is the most convenient way to diversify out of the U.S. dollar and into the Swiss franc. Swiss annuities are backed by substantial Swiss insurance companies. You pay no Swiss withholding tax on your earned interest and your annuity is safe from creditors and lawsuits. As with U.S. annuities, Swiss annuities are tax deferred. I will recommend some specific Swiss annuities later in this chapter.

2) The Japanese yen

The Japanese yen also enjoyed a spectacular run against the dollar in the past decade. The yen rose about 75 percent during the 1980's. But this should not be surprising. During this time, Japan's industrial productivity increased 200 percent! Still, the Japanese yen's stellar performance is not so much because of Japan's industrial prowess as Japan's attitude: unlike the U.S., the Japanese do not manipulate their currency. Their goal is to produce superior products and ignore the strength of the currency that pays for those goods. The Japanese see themselves as producers—not investors. Their formula seems to be working quite well.

Some economists forecast a short-term recession for Japan. It may come. But if it does, it should not seriously depress the yen. I am convinced that over the long term, the yen will continue to comfortably outpace the dollar.

CAUTION

But watch your timing when you invest in Japan because Japan may have short-term troubles. Taiwan, Korea, China and even some South American producers will outperform Japan as the world's low-price producer. Japan must also overcome an enormous trade surplus, which dipped certain Japanese stocks 50 percent or more. I expect further drops. However, in the long run, Japanese securities—and their yen—will rebound and prove to be excellent investments.

3) The Austrian schilling

Third place goes to the Austrian schilling. Why should the schilling get high marks? Because Austria's central bank monetary policy combines stability with a sound interest-rate policy.

That's why schilling deposits rose 750 percent over the past 25 years—out-performing even the Swiss franc by 50 percent!

Another plus for Austria: strong economic ties to the German mark and the Swiss franc. The stability of these two currencies will automatically continue to buoy the Austrian schilling—as long as their cross-rate arrangements continue.

4) The German mark (DEM)

The Deutsche mark has not become the driving force of the European market, as many speculators expected. The DEM has only slightly outperformed the Swiss franc and the U.S. dollar.

What makes the DEM so attractive is its long-term potential. A unified Germany means a far stronger Germany, and this means a stronger DEM. But as with the yen, the DEM's short-term prospects may be shaky because of Germany's enormous reunification costs. Nevertheless, Germany will be the economic center of a Common Market Europe and this must escalate the strength of the DEM over most other European currencies.

These are the four super-performers I recommend, but don't let them blind you to other offshore opportunities.

Europe, for instance, is now one huge success story because of the emerging new Germany and the establishment of the European Common Market. An exceptionally strong European economy means strong currencies for most European countries. This will be the rule for another 10 to 20 years.

> You do not have to buy specific currencies to exploit this European currency boom.

You can buy one currency that includes all the European Common Market currencies—the so-called European Currency Unit, or ECU. The ECU has been around for years but is becoming even more popular now that the European economy is poised to skyrocket. Two more currencies to watch are the Hong Kong and Singapore dollars. Both have strong growth potential. The Pacific rim nations as a whole should do well. The Latin American countries also will come into their own by the year 2000. Our NAFTA trade agreements with Mexico will certainly bolster the peso.

There are also currencies to avoid. One is Canada with a weak economy, high taxes, shaky politics and a poor investment climate. The Canadian dollar will continue to do poorly against the American dollar. The New Zealand and Australian dollars are closer to investment quality but still lack the potential of other currencies.

There are many emerging nations that will benefit greatly from relaxed trade treaties and their currencies may temporarily rise against the dollar. They will not, however, have the economic strength or political stability to sustain their position.

It really is a game. Today's good currency may be tomorrow's bad currency. Then there is the U.S. dollar.

> *note* Trading currencies, like stocks, takes timing, research and luck.

Your savings. CDs. Money market funds. Your cash value life insurance. The money in your pocket. U.S. dollars!

That's the problem. Unless you are one of those farsighted individuals with a foreign bank account or investments—everything you own is in U.S. dollars.

Holding all your wealth in U.S. dollars will be hazardous to your financial health. Unbelievably hazardous!

Consider a few warnings:

- The United States controlled over half of the world's economy in 1970. We now control less than one-third. We are still declining in economic influence. In the very near future, we will control less than one-fifth the world's economy.

- Meanwhile, the U.S. dollar lost 50 percent or more of its value against other currencies such as the Japanese yen, Swiss franc, Austrian schilling and German mark. As American influence on the global economy falters, other economies ascend. Expect the dollar to lose value faster—and lose against many more currencies.

- America, once the leading industrial power, now trails in most major industries: automotive, textiles, computers and consumer electronics, to name a few.

- The U.S. is no longer the world's banker—although we still support too many nations. We are now a debtor nation. Our trade balance is perilous. And our national debt defies mathematical measure and grows bigger daily.

The U.S. dollar is still the world's reserve currency; however, our once-strong global dominance has materially weakened in less than two decades. As we become more of a debtor nation, we can expect more taxes and more inflation—and enough economic instability to drive even the most patriotic American offshore.

Today the U.S. economic outlook remains gloomy. The current disinflation should not cloak the inevitability of a resurgent inflation. Bigger budget deficits will cause our politicians to do what they have always done—hike taxes and confiscate assets in a vain effort to keep the country out of bankruptcy. Eventually there will be exchange controls to prevent assets from moving to a more stable country or currency.

Unless the trend changes—and changes quickly and decisively—the dollar will drop in value against the world's currencies. As a citizen of the world, you will then have less spending power. That is something you cannot afford!

HOT spot A devalued U.S. currency simply makes you poorer.

Hello again to high interest rates

I am tired of a paltry one and one-half percent interest rate from my neighborhood bank. Millions of Americans, particularly fixed-income folks who need their interest income to stay afloat, look at their interest checks with absolute disbelief. That's why more and more Americans now bank overseas where they can get the 10 and 12 percent interest rates their American bankers once paid. For instance, U.S. Treasury bills now pay about four percent. British T-bills pay over 10 percent.

> **note** American banks pay embarrassingly lower interest than banks do in most offshore havens.

Why does interest vary so greatly among countries? One reason is the perceived safety of investment. Another is supply and demand. On both scores, the offshore havens are beating the United States, and beating us badly!

Whatever the reasons for higher offshore interest rates, Americans who can no longer earn the interest rates of the 1980's now happily bank with British, Swiss, Hong Kong or Cayman bankers who pay twice what U.S. bankers pay. Are you a gambler? Nicaraguan banks pay up to 500 percent annual interest—if you don't mind a shaky investment! A high-interest haven can easily double your money in five years. If their currency holds strong against the dollar, your investment can quadruple! This frequently happens to savvy investors.

HOT spot Offshore banks offer a double bonus—higher interest plus an appreciating currency.

Consider interest rates and currency valuation together. One country may pay less interest but have a much stronger currency. You are interested only in the total amount you can eventually repatriate to America. This sum is represented by the accrued interest and the conversion rate of the currency against the U.S. dollar.

As with any investment, there are always trade-offs. You may find offshore banks that pay higher interest are less safe. But this is not always true. Nor do all offshore banks pay considerably more than American banks. Banks in some European havens may pay even less. So you must shop for those good rates. You must also consider banking charges.

But on balance, I believe most Americans with $100,000 or more in U.S. banks should consider shifting at least part of their savings to an offshore bank, so that their blended interest keeps them ahead of inflation.

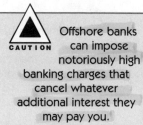

CAUTION Offshore banks can impose notoriously high banking charges that cancel whatever additional interest they may pay you.

Super-growth international stocks and mutual funds

The myth is that the strongest, fastest growing stocks are found on the New York or American stock exchanges. This is no longer true! Just as the highest-yielding bonds, CDs and growth currencies are found overseas—so too are the super-growth international stocks and mutual funds.

In 1971 the U.S. Stock Exchange represented 67 percent of the total global corporate worldwide capitalization. It is now 28 percent. Upstart Japan now controls over 40 percent. The once obscure Seoul, Frankfurt and Singapore stock exchanges now threaten America's corporate leadership. Where will it end?

note Only 26 of the world's largest corporations are American, and most of these are losing ground.

The point is that you can no longer assume the best stocks are American, or that all the action is on Wall Street. You must be a global investor if you want real action.

Nearly every American pension plan now invests heavily overseas.

I am not alone in offering this advice. Half or more of their portfolios are invested overseas for greater appreciation and reduced risk. The pension plans not only diversify broadly among companies and industries to spread their risk but also diversify globally among a wide number of nations.

You will find it more difficult to invest offshore than to bank offshore because most American brokers are unfamiliar with foreign securities, and the smaller brokerage firms cannot directly access the foreign exchanges. It is also more expensive to be an offshore trader. Six to eight percent commissions are common, but the fees are more than offset by the growth potential of these investments.

How do you pick super-growth foreign securities? The answer is that you don't. You instead buy one or more international mutual funds that let you own dozens of global companies selected by the world's most sophisticated and successful portfolio managers. The companies in these funds usually come from high-growth industries and many different countries.

With an international mutual fund, your wealth is safely diversified as you capture profits from some of the world's most exciting companies—whether it be a Portuguese telecommunications company or a Burmese cement producer.

You can choose from literally thousands of excellent funds. The Templeton Emerging Markets Fund, the T. Rowe Price International Stock or Bond Funds and the Scudder International Fund are three excellent examples. But there are many other good funds. Shares of Templeton Emerging Markets Funds are traded on the New York and Pacific stock exchanges under the symbol EMF.

H
I
N
T
You will also find some interesting offshore funds that help you in several innovative ways. For instance, you can buy the Blanchard Short-Term Global Income Fund (800-688-7904). That invests in high-quality, fixed-income global investments with yields 50 percent above what you would get in the United States. Best of all, you have a checkbook so you have instant liquidity!

One easy way to track the performance of these and other international funds is to subscribe to *Barron's/Lipper Mutual Funds Quarterly*. Other investment magazines, such as *Money, Kiplinger's* and *Worth*, also spotlight the offshore funds. Are you a more serious investor? *Morningstar Mutual Funds* will give you a more in depth analysis of a number of offshore funds.

Christopher Weber's and Leonard Reiso's *Getting Rich Outside the Dollar* (Warner Books, 1994) superbly profiles some of the best international funds. This is one book you must read if you want to become a truly knowledgeable international investor. I recommend it.

How to buy offshore funds

As you would expect, the IRS discourages international investing by U.S. citizens, so it makes these investments less attractive to U.S. investors than to foreigners.

But U.S. securities law is the main obstacle. Investment contracts sold within the United States must first be registered with both the Securities and Exchange Commission and the state where it is sold. This, however, can be prohibitively expensive to a foreign mutual fund. U.S. securities laws also demand more detailed disclosure than do the securities laws of most other countries. Few offshore mutual funds will invest the time and expense necessary to comply with these unduly restrictive U.S. securities laws with a dismal track record for preventing securities fraud. Surprisingly, several top mutual funds are still operated by Americans from the United States, but they do not accept investments from U.S. residents. They sell only to foreigners to avoid these registration costs and legal restrictions.

U.S. citizens circumvent these regulatory obstacles by buying international mutual funds through offshore bank accounts, international companies or business trusts. You can travel overseas to buy the shares personally, invest through a foreign bank account or establish a foreign trust or company as the investor. Offshore mutual funds cannot directly accept money from a U.S. investor but can, for instance, sell to the U.S. investor's foreign trust or company.

Because you will probably want to diversify your international portfolio, you should also invest in the international funds of a U.S.-based mutual fund, as do many U.S. investors. Besides having operated longer than U.S. funds, offshore mutual funds (or unit trusts, as they are called overseas) have shown superior long-term performance and boast more experienced management. And

Offshore trustees or company directors will invest for you, as you direct, so you retain complete control over your investments.

because they are free of U.S. securities laws, they maintain lower operating costs which produce higher yields.

Offshore mutual funds are usually classified either as "accumulative" or "roll-up" funds. Under U.S. tax law, a mutual fund avoids taxes on its income

note Offshore mutual funds offer very attractive tax benefits under foreign tax laws, but pose problems for U.S. taxpayers.

and capital gains by annually distributing its profits to its shareholders who are then taxed on these earnings. Offshore havens can generally retain and compound their income and gains. So while taxes deplete a U.S. investors' investments each year, overseas investors enjoy tax-deferred investments—and thus faster accumulation of their investment portfolio.

Other countries tax a fund investor's accumulated income and capital gains, but only when the shares are redeemed. Some havens never tax the capital gains, or tax gains at a far lower tax rate than does the United States. A U.S. taxpayer who invests offshore can reap these tax benefits. The tax on redeemed shares may even be exempt from tax withholding if there is a tax treaty between the United States and that country.

The many attractive investment advantages available to Americans from the offshore mutual funds cannot be overlooked. Yet, international diversification, strong performance and solid management become only a small part of their story. The big plus is that you have an investment that compounds tax-free until you redeem your shares and an offshore mutual fund that essentially becomes an unlimited IRA or tax-deferred annuity.

Uncle Sam continuously tries to erode the advantages that beckon money to offshore havens. But loopholes can still be found. For instance, until 1986, the United States taxed U.S. shareholders with foreign investment funds the same way foreign countries taxed their citizens: taxes were paid only when the shares were redeemed. To tighten our laws, the U.S. then deferred taxes only when 50 percent or more of the shareholders in the fund were foreigners.

Under present U.S. tax law, there are only two ways left for Americans to solve the offshore mutual funds tax problem. One way is to invest in a "qualified electing fund" or an offshore investment company that elects to tax its shareholders annually on their earnings. Of course, few offshore mutual funds are "qualified electing funds" because their stockholders would automatically lose the big benefit of tax deferments, and the foreign fund would then be on par with American funds. Another alternative is to defer the taxes until you redeem your shares. The problem here is that you must then pay both the regular income tax plus a penalty tax, or an extra interest charge for not paying taxes on the income and gains in the year earned.

This tax disadvantage discourages many Americans from offshore mutual fund investing. But even with this tax problem, offshore mutual fund investing is still very advantageous because the IRS interest rate (currently only three percent more than the federal short-term rate) is not due until after the shares are redeemed or an "excess distribution" is received by the stockholder. Meanwhile, you benefit from tax-deferred compounding. A high-yield mutual fund that gives you tax-deferred compounding still outweighs the penalty charge—particularly if the shares are held long term.

A third alternative to avoid the tax problem is to own your mutual fund shares through a decontrolled foreign corporation, or an offshore company with substantial non-subpart F income. You can also use any other legal entity that prevents an income pass-through to U.S. shareholders.

Still another alternative is not to redeem your fund shares but pass them onto your heirs whose tax basis on the shares will be their market value when you die. Since your heirs' tax basis is the shares' new fair market value, your heirs will have no appreciable taxable capital gain.

A final possibility. Own your mutual shares through an offshore trust throughout your lifetime. Upon your death the trust will no longer have a U.S. citizen as grantor so the shares can be redeemed without any capital gain pass-through to your estate. Meanwhile, the trust reinvests its income. Review these tax strategies with your U.S. tax adviser, because you can easily run afoul of the U.S. tax laws.

Offshore annuities

Offshore annuities generally give you the same big advantage as U.S. annuities: tax-deferred income compounding until you sell. Offshore annuity payments are taxed by the IRS the same way as U.S. annuity policies are taxed. But, the offshore insurance company that sells annuities to Americans must have an option letter

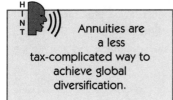

Annuities are a less tax-complicated way to achieve global diversification.

to certify that the annuity meets U.S. tax-deferral requirements. Annuities also offer tax advantages offshore. Non-residents ordinarily do not pay income, capital gains or inheritance taxes on the annuity.

What I like most about offshore annuities is that they are creditor protected and provide considerable privacy. Foreign annuities are not reportable on your tax returns as are foreign bank accounts. U.S. creditors cannot normally seize an offshore annuity managed by a foreign trustee. Nor can you lose the annuity in bankruptcy. Some states, such as Florida, specifically exempt all annuities from creditor claims—whether the annuities are foreign or domestic.

Finally, an annuity may trade in the funds or securities from a wide range of countries. This is truly global investing at its best.

I usually recommend Swiss annuities because they are "no-load," can be canceled anytime without penalty or loss of principal, and are exempt from the 35 percent Swiss withholding tax on interest payments.

Swiss annuities can be purchased by U.S. tax-sheltered pension plans, Keoughs, IRAs, and similar corporate plans. Or these plans can be rolled over into a Swiss annuity. All that is required is the appointment of a U.S. trustee to hold the annuity contract. Most American banks will fulfill that trustee role for a small administrative fee.

Swiss annuities can be canceled at any time without penalty (other than a small penalty in the first year). Moreover, there are no front-end or back-end loads.

Swiss annuities, including the popular Swiss Plus, give about the same return as long-term government bonds. While this is not a spectacular return, it is more than adequate, considering the several tax and non-tax advantages they offer.

Good annuities can be found in virtually every haven, and many promise considerably greater yields than can be obtained with Swiss annuities. Unless the insurance company selling the annuity is exceptionally well-rated, it is best to accept the safety of the Swiss annuity—even if it means a more modest return.

Gold plan

No discussion of offshore investing would be complete without mention of Gold Plan—a unique gold investment program sponsored by the Swiss Uberseebank. If you want to take advantage of gold's investment and insurance benefits without actually buying gold bullion directly, then investigate Gold Plan.

How to start your offshore investment program

 Investing offshore follows the same fundamental rules that you would follow when investing here at home. How can you start to take advantage of the exceptional investment opportunities offshore? Here are six tips:

1) Learn all you can about the offshore investment opportunities before you invest. Read the financial journals. Call for a prospectus from the underwriters I mention in this chapter—and others who have financial products of interest to you. Protection only comes through knowledge!

2) Decide on the amount you will invest offshore. First, of course, you must decide how much you will invest anywhere, after considering your financial needs. You must then decide how much you will invest onshore versus offshore. A good rule of thumb: The more you have to invest, the more you should invest offshore.

3) Deal with offshore brokers who are familiar with U.S. tax laws.

4) Stay with safe offshore investments. Avoid the more speculative financial

Hire a good American financial advisor who is knowledgeable about offshore investments.

products that constantly flourish from the less-developed havens. Favor the European, particularly the Swiss, investments.

5) Buy offshore investments that best meet your financial objectives. Remember, offshore investments are as diverse as the reasons for investing.

6) Diversify. Don't put all your eggs in one offshore basket.

Key points to remember

◆ Americans with wealth can no longer rely on the American economy to insure their financial future.

◆ The United States dollar is losing ground against other currencies—and this is eroding your wealth.

◆ Diversification has always been the key to investment safety. Today that means geographic diversification.

◆ Offshore banks do pay higher interest rates than American banks—but you must watch the risk.

◆ The offshore mutual funds are the global super-performers. And these are offshore funds for virtually every American investor!

◆ Swiss annuities are one of the best investments for American investors. They offer an unbeatable combination of tax and non-tax advantages.

◆ A sound offshore investment program is designed the same way as a domestic investment program—with knowledge, caution and a clear sense of purpose.

How to become financially invisible offshore

4

Chapter 4

How to become financially invisible offshore

Offshore financial freedom has traditionally been the lure of financial privacy. The search for secrecy and privacy still motivate countless Americans to expatriate their money offshore. They feel, as I do, that in today's America—and in most countries—individual privacy no longer exists. What little remains, we are rapidly losing. Those who believe it is their absolute right—and an absolute necessity—to keep their financial affairs completely confidential soon realize that this is only possible when their wealth is offshore. Only the offshore havens have secrecy laws that acknowledge privacy as everyone's inherent right—and a right to be protected at all costs.

A world of snoops

We no longer guarantee it to our citizens. In fact, our laws are designed to expose our financial affairs to just about any snoop wishing to pry: litigants, creditors, the IRS, ex-spouses, prospective heirs, even competitors and business associates to name a few. Under the false flags of national

note America no longer prizes privacy.

security and crime prevention, our beloved Uncle Sam has progressively poked holes in the once-staunch walls of financial privacy. Today's predatory society makes it more critical than ever to maintain a low financial profile. It also makes it more difficult, if not impossible.

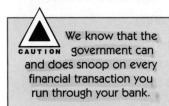

CAUTION We know that the government can and does snoop on every financial transaction you run through your bank.

Not too many years ago it was different. Our right to privacy was guaranteed by our Constitution's Bill of Rights. The First Amendment's freedom of speech implied the right to be protected against Big Brother's unwanted intrusions.

Financial privacy is also implicitly secured by the Fifth Amendment. It provides "no citizen shall be compelled, in any criminal case, to bear witness against himself, nor be deprived of life, liberty or property, without due process of law." But does this protection from self-incrimination stop criminal tax investigators, the SEC or other regulators or prosecutors from seizing your financial and personal records so they can be used against you in a criminal case? Of course not.

The courts recognize that private records can be incriminating but only narrowly protect them. Court rulings consistently hold that the only constitutionally protected records are "private records"—those in your possession. Financial records in the possession of your U.S. banks, investment brokers, accountants, financial planners or other third parties (except your lawyer) are unprotected and can be summoned for investigation or trial even if illegally obtained.

If you still think you are safe from government snoops, then here are a few more sorry examples to show how your privacy has all but disappeared:

- Our own U.S. Supreme Court recently ruled that the police and other law enforcement agencies, including the IRS, can search your rubbish for damaging evidence. No search warrant is needed—as long as the rubbish is not on your property.

- The U.S. Treasury Department is building a fast-growing, detailed data bank on every American with a foreign bank account. Fortunately, it still cannot discover what's in the bank.

> **HOT spot** The SEC can enter your investment advisor's office and examine your files without your investment advisor's consent or a search warrant.

- The U.S. Passport Office developed a new machine-readable passport to more closely monitor air travel to and from the U.S. This particularly includes travel to and from the offshore havens.

- Every U.S. government agency now utilizes advanced technologies, and the expanded legal right to snoop on telephone conversations, particularly those involving financial crimes.

We can point to an avalanche of cases where our government has intruded into the deepest recesses of a citizen's personal or financial affairs. If you want to see for yourself how closely Uncle Sam scrutinizes what you do with your money, then I suggest you subscribe to the Privacy Report. It's essential reading for every American who prizes his privacy rights! Another revealing book on the subject is Mark Skousen's, The Complete Guide to Financial Privacy. They say essentially the same thing: financial privacy in America no longer exists!

As a lawyer, I am bewildered by this rapid erosion of our basic right to privacy. As an American, it saddens me. But in our imperfect world it doesn't pay to dwell on matters you cannot change. It's smarter to control events and take things into your own hands. Only then can you gain the secrecy you are entitled to—even if that must be found beyond our borders. That's what you will learn to do in this chapter.

Your bank—the spy

Let's start where financial privacy should be most rigidly guarded—your bank. Unfortunately, the banking secrecy that Americans can expect in the United States is murky. On one hand, bankers are ethically bound to maintain the confidentiality of their depositors' affairs, and some states prohibit all but reasonable disclosures. Still, American banks are deluged daily with requests from businesses, individuals and law enforcement agencies requesting information about depositors.

The release of information is normally viewed as a courtesy to a depositor: confirmatory information that allows the depositor to obtain credit, open an account elsewhere or make an investment. With little or no hesitation, any bank will reveal whether the depositor has an account, for how long, if the banking relationship is satisfactory, and there have been sufficient funds to cover checks.

American bankers could always refuse to volunteer information to private sources, unless they were armed with a subpoena. Bankers had less choice in the matter when the requests for information come from the government. Case law clearly gave federal and state investigators legal rights to a depositor's records, and the subpoena could always be used when the bank was less cooperative.

In 1970, Congress passed the Bank Secrecy Act that requires all U.S. banks to maintain duplicate records of their customers' financial transactions. The Secrecy Act was designed to insure that details of every banking transaction would be forever available to government snoops. Specifically, the law requires banks to make:

1) A microfilm or other reproduction of each check, draft or similar instrument drawn upon it and presented to it for payment; and

2) A record of each check, draft, or similar instrument received by it for deposit or collection, together with an identification of the party for whose account it is to be deposited or collected.

The audacity of our government to entitle the law the "Bank Secrecy Act" insults the intelligence of thinking Americans because the law does exactly the opposite of what its name suggests. Not surprisingly, the U.S. Supreme Court continued its longstanding record of thrashing individual rights and expanding governmental powers and upheld the law's constitutionality in the infamous U.S. vs. Miller case. The court curiously reasoned that "bank customers whose records are sought by the government—for whatever reason—have no right to [expect] that access is controlled by an existing legal process." That sums up our government's attitude about your right to privacy.

note

Uncle Sam recruited your bank to be its very own super-spy against you!

Flushed with this new and expanded power to snoop, federal agencies and prosecutors quickly flooded the nation's banks with subpoenas. Private litigants gained near-automatic access to their opponent's most sensitive financial records. American banks, once a bastion of confidentiality, reluctantly surrendered any claim that they could shelter their depositors' privacy.

This loss of banking secrecy extends even to those not directly involved in a legal case. Third-party records are routinely subpoenaed from banks when they are thought to contain information even remotely connected to the case.

This open door policy to banking records significantly increased the number of prosecutions and convictions for federal and state crimes. Most were tax violations. But it also made each of us less secure about things we once considered confidential.

To its small credit, Congress slightly closed the door on the nose of government snoops by enacting the Tax Reform Act of 1976 (TEFRA). TEFRA lets bank customers challenge an IRS attempt to seize their bank records. But the law gives the IRS big loopholes because people "suspected" of a crime have no right to challenge the seizure. Since the word "suspected" is not defined, the IRS can, with impunity, grab records in contravention of TEFRA's intent simply by claiming that suspicion. In essence, this means you can do little or nothing if your bank records are seized by a law enforcement agency. The Financial Privacy Act of 1978 also gave U.S. citizens more protection because the federal government must now notify you beforehand and give you the opportunity to challenge its search of your bank records. This law also extends to records held by savings and loan associations and credit card companies.

But challenging a search is usually futile. In practice, the law hardly prevents searches. More accurately, the law only requires you

note The courts quite liberally allow the government to search.

be informed about the search. Many banks ignore the law and, without notice to their customers, let the government access records, frequently with devastating results to their customers.

As the government's super-spy, U.S. banks also must maintain records on every check you write over $100, as well as cash transactions (deposits and withdrawals) over $10,000. Banks also must record all credit transactions over $5,000.

So they can better spy, you cannot open a bank account without giving the bank your Social Security number or taxpayer ID number. If you fail to, your account is automatically inspected by the IRS after 90 days. The question is—why should you pay your bank hefty fees and charges to handle your banking business when it is working full- time as Uncle Sam's super-snoop?

The naked American

Does the government really need more spies? Our federal government now has about 25 files on you—if you are that average American. They have 200 or more files on some Americans. Their mammoth computer system can instantly reveal virtually everything the government could possibly want to know about you—including your finances.

For instance, the IRS closely tabs your income. Then comes an army of other federal agencies: the Social Security Administration, the armed forces, the agency that gave you a business or student loan—hundreds of alphabet agencies, each with its own growing dossier on you. Why this compelling effort to rob us of our privacy? After all, only a comparatively tiny handful of Americans are big-time tax evaders, drug dealers, illegal stock traders or organized crime chieftains.

Uncle Sam does not need to dig too deeply for the dirt on your business or personal financial goings-on.

But even when Big Brother snoops on their finances, it nevertheless robs those law-abiding citizens who do not fear public disclosure of their privacy rights.

note

Financial privacy is critical if you want to keep your personal assets concealed from those who are after them.

This mandatory exposure of our finances to the government also forces exposure of our finances to private litigants. Nearly every American periodically gets embroiled in a nasty divorce, a serious lawsuit or a family dispute.

You still need financial privacy even if your assets are not threatened. You may want your investments and money matters kept confidential for personal reasons. Your investments may carry political overtones. Your past financial dealings could hurt your reputation. You may have managed your wealth poorly, and this could cost you your job or career.

Financial privacy can also help you protect yourself from crime. Visible wealth attracts swindlers, gold-diggers, ne'er-do-well family members, shady promoters and society's other parasites and vultures. You must keep your wealth invisible today!

note

Yet, anyone can get a quick-fix on your wealth. It's remarkably easy. Public records reveal mountains of information about you. Countless private firms called "asset locators" find and reveal an individual's or company's assets. These firms work primarily for lawyers and judgment creditors, but they also uncover assets in divorce cases and for other civil matters. For a modest fee they will deliver, to anyone willing to pay their fee, a fairly accurate financial profile on you.

One such company, International Intelligence Network Corp., monitors an individual's personal and financial data for private institutions, as well as federal and state law enforcement agencies, including the IRS. This firm

HOT *spot* Computers strip bare every American because computers leave few transactions unrecorded.

conducts "Public Information and Asset Tracking" seminars and teaches attendees how to obtain more than 50 different financial facts on anyone—searching only the public records.

But those who search public records are behind the times. Our new computers make it unnecessary to probe public records. Once confidential, financial information is now available with a push of a button. Whenever you apply for credit, cash a check, make a major purchase, seek employment or open a bank account—you provide financial information. So, too, do your other financial reports.

You are a very naked American!

Secret money havens

Thus, the sorry fact is that we have no true privacy in America—or even the right to privacy. Our financial life is completely exposed through public records. What is not publicly exposed is easily obtained through summons, subpoena or simple request.

That is why I say the U.S. is an unfriendly place for any individual or company anxious for true financial privacy. Very unfriendly. Others agree. That is, of course, another reason the offshore havens have become so attractive. They deliver true secrecy, privacy and freedom from intrusion. The havens give your private affairs what our forefathers once promised us and our contemporary politicians and Supreme Court have so cavalierly taken away. In fact, the havens deliver more privacy than we were ever promised here in America.

There have always been those who hid their wealth; whether from family members, business partners, neighbors, thieves or the government. Hollow tree trunks, mattresses, buried chests, caves, loose bricks in the walls, and other treasure troves have, for centuries, served this need for secrecy. In the financial secrecy business—as with all businesses—demand creates its own supply.

The modernization of currency transactions made international banking a feasible alternative. Some countries decided they could replace the hole in the ground or stuffed mattress and deliver a secrecy unobtainable in the wealth-holder's own country. Selling secrecy brought income and profits to the secrecy haven and privacy to its foreign depositors. It was a win-win situation. That was the game plan then, and that is the game plan now.

note Offshore banks have become the best way to protect privacy.

With privacy and confidentiality part of the offshore advantage, and their stock in trade (along with asset protection, good investments and tax avoidance), they tighten their privacy laws to outdo other havens and attract even more privacy-seeking investors.

Secrecy offshore is accomplished in one of two ways. First, havens enact domestic bank secrecy laws which keep bank records absolutely protected—whether against governments or private parties. Second are the blocking statutes which prohibit the disclosure, copying, inspection or removal of documents—even under foreign court order. This also prevents the taking of deposition or the subpoena of witnesses within the haven.

 If you deposit your money in havens with strong secrecy laws, you will enjoy virtually complete financial privacy. Absolutely protected are your:

- bank records and banking transactions

- books, records and correspondence between yourself and your professional advisors

- records of communications and transactions with common carriers

This guarantee of privacy and confidentiality also extends to your agents, employees, directors, customers, and all others involved with your offshore banking.

Most havens impose very strict penalties on secrecy law violators. Bankers, in some havens, can be imprisoned for up to ten years for secrecy law violations. And they do not give privacy law enforcement lip service. Offshore bankers do go to jail! This contrasts sharply with the U.S. where bankers go to jail for not snitching on their depositors. Moreover, in many havens, a depositor can sue a banker who violates the privacy law.

> *note*
> Offshore havens make it illegal for a bank to violate the secrecy laws.

It is important to understand that in the better havens, this right to privacy is absolute. No government agency can compel disclosure. No court can compel disclosure. There is no legal process by which disclosure

> **HOT spot** Privacy is guaranteed even if the inquiry involves criminal or tax violations.

can be forced. Only the depositor himself can waive his privacy rights and allow disclosure. And a bank can disclose absolutely no information. It is illegal for a bank to say whether or not a person is a depositor or customer. Nor does it matter why disclosure is sought.

But privacy offshore cannot be taken for granted. Several once-excellent secrecy havens no longer guarantee secrecy. Their trademark of privacy is long-tarnished, and there are too many cracks in their walls.

Switzerland, for example, was traditionally ranked as the most secretive of all the havens. But since the early 1980s Switzerland has dangerously relaxed its secrecy standards. You may have seen this in the American prosecutor's ability to get Swiss banking records during the Iran-Contra affair. Philippines President Ferdinand Marcos similarly discovered to his sorrow that "secret" Swiss bank accounts are not always secretive.

Why this erosion in the foreign secrecy laws? One reason is that a haven may begin to prioritize other benefits—such as tax protection or

> ⚠️ **CAUTION** Countries that heavily depend upon U.S. support are poor havens when privacy is your objective.

investments—and gradually shifts away from privacy. You must guard against this privacy erosion when you bank offshore. Havens are like any enterprise, they become sloppy and lose their edge to newer competitors with tighter privacy. You must always monitor your haven's current privacy policies to make certain it gives you the secrecy you want. More often, offshore havens with once-sound secrecy laws accede to U.S. economic, legal or political pressures to relax their privacy.

Many countries, such as Switzerland, drop their veil of secrecy only under circumstances carefully prescribed in their treaty with the United States. Under the U.S.-Swiss treaty, American prosecutors can only get financial information from the Swiss when ample evidence suggests that a crime has occurred. Moreover, it must be a crime under Swiss law. Fortunately, tax evasion is not considered a crime under Swiss law, so the IRS gains little cooperation from the Swiss. Switzerland also gives its depositors the right to petition their government not to reveal requested financial information. Many of these appeals are decided on behalf of the depositor.

Other havens that have tax treaties with the U.S., also have their treaties specify when the haven must release information to the U.S. For instance, the United States has a longstanding tax treaty with the United Kingdom. Still, the British colony havens are among the best tax

> *note* In the absence of clear evidence of a crime—usually drug trafficking or money laundering—Swiss banking secrecy remains airtight.

havens and offer good, if not absolute, secrecy. One advantage of a tax treaty is that it specifies the cooperation—or lack of cooperation—the U.S. can expect concerning an investor's offshore finances.

For instance, the U.S. tax treaty with the British colonies compels cooperation and disclosure only when there is proof of criminal intent on the part of the offshore investor. To safeguard against arbitrary disclosure, the treaty defines "intent" with four pages of painstaking exactness.

The British colonies then, at least can be secretive for those who remain unindicted. The indicted depositor may prefer a haven that holds its secrets under all circumstances.

Which havens prize secrecy the most? My current favorites are Austria, Hungary, the Cook Islands, Netherland Antilles, Antigua, Nevis, the Channel Islands, the Turks and Gibraltar. The Caymans and Bahamas are still reasonably good for privacy. Numbered Swiss accounts are still secretive but not as sound as before.

This does not suggest that other havens are not secretive, or that the recommended secrecy havens provide complete privacy under all circumstances. Secrecy is a comparative term. You must compare the secrecy standards of one haven against all others. One obscure privacy haven is the Kingdom of Tonga, a tiny atoll about 2,000 miles east of Australia. Tonga has exceptionally strong secrecy laws, and to add to its secrecy is the fact that nobody ever heard of Tonga and fewer still know how to find it!

How offshore havens protect privacy

As an American involved in a lawsuit, your U.S. bank must give your opponent subpoenaed banking records. In contrast, offshore records are fully protected from U.S. court orders and subpoenas.

Offshore banks are jurisdictionally immune to service of process. Under no circumstances can an offshore bank divulge financial information about you to any third party—absent treaty provisions to the contrary.

The fact that offshore banks are jurisdictionally immune to service of process is important, because this effectively bans writs of execution or attachment orders. The secrecy laws of most havens not only protect entrusted funds from creditor seizure originating from a domestic judgment, but these same laws also protect the confidentiality of all financial transactions that pass through the bank.

> *note*
> Under no circumstances, including lawsuits or criminal investigations, will an offshore bank disclose protected information.

Moreover, if your offshore bank has no presence in the U.S., through

American-based branches or affiliates, it will not come under the jurisdiction of American courts, and U.S. demands for information will also be barred by American courts if disclosure violates the secrecy laws of the offshore haven. This remains so even if the offshore bank is owned or operated by a U.S. resident, as the offshore bank is considered a separate entity, and one obligated to protect the confidentiality of its depositors.

The secrecy laws of all countries prohibit using the citizenry of a bank's principals to circumvent the privacy law that extends to the offshore bank as a separate entity. This jurisdictional immunity is why offshore banks can guarantee against invasion of your financial privacy. Records so readily obtainable within the U.S. are beyond the reach of prying governmental investigators and private litigants once these records are deposited in the right offshore haven.

Privacy is a big benefit of offshore banking, yet many American investors overlook its importance. But once you consider how exposing your finances can get you into serious trouble, the privacy advantage grows in importance.

Seeking privacy is the right of all free citizens of the world. The fact that so many are in search of privacy does not speak against them, but against their countries who stripped them of their privacy. And you must ignore those who say privacy encourages illegality. Financial privacy for legitimate activities should be the goal of every American offshore investor. No less important is the goal to fight the "open book" laws of the U.S. or other countries that believe your affairs are everyone's business!

Becoming private in a public world

How do you gain financial privacy through offshore havens? You create two separate financial worlds.

Your public world is your home country where you work, pay taxes, keep your bank accounts and those investments and finances you expect the world to know about.

Your private world is offshore—where you keep your "invisible" money—money only you know about.

Within this private world are your major bank accounts, investments, trusts, companies and other entities that are formed to hold assets you want to remain invisible and private.

Keep your two worlds completely separate. There should be absolutely no direct transactions between these two worlds. For example, you should never directly transfer funds from your onshore

The key to secrecy is never to mix your private world with your public world.

(public world) bank to your offshore (private world) bank. Your money can then be easily traced, and you forfeit secrecy. Instead, you must indirectly transfer your funds through one or more intermediaries—such as an offshore company—who will then redeposit it in your offshore account.

For example, suppose you live in New York and want to set up an asset protection trust in the Caymans. Your goal is to secretly transfer $500,000 from your New York banks to your trust accounts in the Caymans. Obviously, if you send a check or wire transfer funds from your New York banks to your Cayman bank, American investigators can easily detect the transfer and the existence of your Cayman account simply by examining the records of your New York accounts. Your American investigators may not find out anything more about your Cayman account, but they do know of its existence—and how much you initially transferred to it.

To break the trail, you may instead wire the funds from New York to an account in the Bahamas and then transfer it from the Bahamas to the Caymans. Because the Bahamian account is protected, the investigators' trail will end there.

You can make it even more difficult for investigators by using offshore companies or international business corporations as intermediaries. For under $300, you may set up a Bahamian company, or a company in virtually any other haven, and funnel the money through this haven.

What happens if you do inadvertently connect your onshore and offshore banks? Start again and open a new offshore account.

It is not necessary to segregate your offshore accounts from each other. Once your money is in one offshore haven, investigators won't discover other offshore accounts because all offshore accounts are shrouded in secrecy. But to directly transfer funds from one offshore account to another does sacrifice some privacy if one haven is less secretive.

For greater diversification and secrecy, you may establish several accounts in one haven. Transfers between these accounts will not destroy secrecy because they are all within the same offshore haven.

To repatriate your money, you must go through the same process in reverse—channel your money back to the United States through one or more offshore intermediary accounts.

How to quietly move your money

The key question is how do you move your money secretly from your public onshore accounts to your private offshore bank? To begin with, you must understand that it is absolutely legal to move your money offshore.

The Bank Secrecy Act of 1970 creates further reporting requirements on anyone (individuals or businesses) who transports monetary instruments across U.S. boundaries.

Monetary instruments, under the law, include U.S. and foreign currency, traveler's checks, and any security or negotiable instrument in bearer form whose value is $10,000 or more. The report is filed on Customs Form 4790. Although the report is filed only with Customs, the information is available to all federal agencies, including the IRS.

Within the two requirements of legality and secrecy, you have several alternatives—each with its own advantages and disadvantages.

Mail is the most common way to transfer funds offshore. You can legally send a check or money order—in any amount—to any offshore haven. While this is the most convenient way to transfer funds, you must observe a few additional tricks to avoid detection.

The first rule is never use a personal check—even to expatriate small amounts. The Secrecy Act requires your bank to record checks above $10,000, but in practice most banks microfilm all checks. Wire transfers are also recorded, so again you lose privacy. Almost all offshore banks accept wire transfers, as most have corresponding banks or foreign exchange dealers to help process the wire transfers. Speed is the only advantage of a wire transfer over mail.

You can directly transfer money market funds by wire to your offshore bank, with your funds only identified by the account number. A letter of instruction to the offshore bank would accompany the funds. This provides more secrecy, but a diligent investigator can still discover the transfer by examining the money market account.

Another possibility is to buy bonds for less than $10,000. Provided the face value is under $10,000, you need not report the transfer to customs. You can mail a bond every day and very quickly build a tidy offshore nest egg. Of course, you must buy the bonds for cash to leave no paper trail.

Sending cash through the mail is also permitted in amounts up to $10,000, but it's not smart to transfer funds this way for obvious reasons. Yet, many people frequently do mail small amounts of cash offshore with surprisingly little loss.

> **HOT spot** Money orders and cashier's checks are the two best ways to mail funds offshore.

If the money order is for more than $10,000, it must be payable to your offshore bank or a specific offshore individual or company. As it is not "bearer" currency, it would not be reportable to Customs. A money order above $10,000 payable to "cash" is bearer currency and, like cash, must be reported to Customs. Money orders under $10,000 may be payable to "cash," provided you send no more than one money order at a time. For maximum secrecy, do not include your name on the money order. Use an accompanying side letter to instruct the bank to deposit the funds to your account.

Use cashier's checks purchased with cash to send larger amounts offshore. This breaks the paper trail. Since the check bears only the bank manager's signature, it will be untraceable to you. As with money orders, cashier's checks over $10,000 must be payable to a specific payee (such as your offshore bank or company) and not "cash"—if you are to avoid reporting to Customs. You can enhance privacy by using a box number, not your address, on accompanying correspondence.

Would you feel safer if your money was personally transported offshore? Many people do, particularly when it is their initial offshore transfer.

To personally carry your money offshore can be expensive and inconvenient, but it is an alternative, and a good one, if you have travel money and your haven can double as a vacation spot. Popular havens are often popular vacation hideaways, so not surprisingly many Americans and Canadians do personally transport their money offshore.

You can also hire a courier to personally transport your funds offshore. Brokerage firms and international banks provide couriers. You can also find private couriers although most do not advertise their services. Some are executives who routinely travel abroad on their own business. Be careful: There are also plenty of criminals and other undesirables who pose as couriers. This explains the heavy losses and thefts that occur with couriers and why I do not recommend their use. Courier service can be expensive. Typically they charge a minimum fee of $1,000 or 5 percent of the funds transported, whichever is higher.

Remember: you only avoid Customs reporting if you take offshore less than $10,000 in cash, bearer instruments, money orders or traveler's checks per individual per trip. If you travel with a spouse or friend, you can each carry under $10,000 without Customs reporting. You are not limited to the number of times you can travel abroad; however, Uncle Sam is beginning to oversee travel through computerized passport tracking. So if you do plan frequent trips offshore, it is wise to get a second passport to lessen the chance of a tax audit.

> **HINT** Commodities are not subject to the reporting requirements.

Another popular strategy is to carry precious commodities offshore. Once offshore, commodities such as diamonds, rare coins or gold, can easily be converted to funds for deposit.

International transactions usually do not involve cash but are only intangible computer entries via telephone, telex or telecopier. This points out that it is remarkably easy to bank offshore and, with a little advance planning, can be done in a way that will guarantee total privacy.

How to secretly retrieve your money

No matter why or where you send your money, the time will eventually arrive when you will want all or part of it home again where you can spend it. How do you achieve this? You reverse the process used to send money offshore.

You may also repatriate up to $10,000 at a time in cash or bearer currency without Customs notification. This is a practical alternative if you frequently visit your haven.

You can also have your offshore haven bank wire you the funds through "pay by identification." You need only satisfactorily identify yourself to the recipient U.S. bank to retrieve your money. This does not promote secrecy if it directly links your two financial worlds. For that reason, you must wire the funds through your intermediary accounts and entities.

A more convenient way to repatriate your funds is to have your offshore bank send you frequent bank drafts on the account of its American correspondent banks. Most offshore banks have correspondents in major U.S. cities.

If you want to maintain privacy or protect your funds from your creditors, then you do not want your funds deposited to a U.S. bank account under your name. One solution is to cash the check at the correspondent bank. Or have your offshore bank send you bearer securities under $10,000. Your offshore-bank can also transmit funds (rare coins are recommended) to a U.S. collectibles dealer who accepts the check in exchange for coins or some other collectible.

If asset protection is another goal, your repatriated funds must continuously remain under another name to stay safe from your creditors. One strategy is to set up a Nevada or Wyoming corporation to receive the funds. The ownership in corporations organized in these states is undocumented. Or you may title the repatriated funds with a family limited partnership in which you own a minor interest. Are you happily married? Wiring the funds to your spouse's account may be another answer. You can also have the offshore funds

transferred to a domestic spendthrift trust with yourself as beneficiary. A spendthrift trust prevents your creditors from reaching your beneficial interest.

If an asset is transferred offshore, you may bring it back to the United States without tax consequences, provided it has not increased in value. When repatriated, gains or profits are taxed as interest, capital gains, or dividends.

Claim your right to privacy

Why privacy? Its purpose is not because you are doing something wrong or have something to hide. The fact that you seek privacy implies nothing more than you prefer the world not know your business. That is how it should be. Unfortunately, it is a right you must work at to reclaim. Just as unfortunate, you must find your privacy outside the United States.

Key points to remember

◆ In today's predatory world, you cannot keep your affairs public. You need privacy.

◆ We are constantly losing our privacy and new technology and laws that expand the rights of government to snoop on our affairs make it more difficult to keep our affairs public.

◆ Virtually every transaction that goes through your bank is open for government inspection. Larger transactions are automatically reported to the IRS.

◆ Most offshore havens guarantee their depositors some degree of financial privacy. In many havens, secrecy is absolute.

◆ To maintain privacy, it is important not to leave a paper trail that can lead snoops to your offshore accounts.

Building your offshore financial fortress

5

Chapter 5

Building your offshore financial fortress

A frequently ignored benefit of the offshore haven is its great ability to protect your personal and business assets. Shrewd Americans, and other nationals, know they must protect themselves from:

note Asset protection is a chief reason people transfer their wealth offshore.

- **Lawsuits:** Over 50 million lawsuits are filed each year in the United States. The overwhelming odds are that you'll face at least one killer lawsuit in the next four years.

- **The IRS:** 20 million Americans owe back taxes to the IRS. Savvy tax delinquents have discovered the IRS is powerless to seize money overseas.

- **Creditors:** Offshore havens can be the only safe money refuge—even if you must file bankruptcy.

- **Spouses or ex-spouses:** one of every two marriages ends in divorce. Asset protection via the offshore haven is an increasingly popular maneuver for the soon-to-be-divorced.

RICO and other draconian federal statutes allow Uncle Sam to grab your assets without notice or court order.

There are other reasons to protect your assets. Perhaps you seek protection from arbitrary and capricious governmental seizures. If you are not aware that the government has you targeted, they can seize your money and other onshore assets before you even know that you are in trouble! So you must protect your assets before you need protection. Later may be too late!

Face the facts: in today's lawsuit-crazy, high-risk world the bigger challenge is not making money but keeping it. Survivors find offshore havens are their one best financial fortress because that is where the strongest financial fortresses are built.

Unfortunately, we live in an imperfect world, a world where we are victimized by circumstances and dilemmas that were never planned and certainly not welcomed.

An offshore haven is the only safe alternative once somebody is already in pursuit of your money. Protective transfers to hinder or delay existing creditors can be set aside as fraudulent transfers. While it also may be a fraudulent transfer to shelter your money offshore and put it beyond the reach of creditors, it is, nevertheless, a transfer that your creditors and the courts cannot revoke.

CAUTION Once someone has a claim against you, it is usually too late to rely upon domestic asset protection strategies.

People who are sued or have the tax collector after them increasingly protect their wealth in offshore havens. Whether it is a malpractice suit, a motor vehicle accident case, a damage suit for injuries around the home or business, a negligence claim, a breach of contract lawsuit, huge medical bills, regulatory liability, or to protect property in a dissolving marriage, the offshore haven can be your best defense!

 It is also not smart to think you can hide your assets if someone gets a judgment against you. Once there is a judgment against you, the court will compel you to disclose, under oath, every last asset you own or have owned in the preceding five years. You must tell the court everything—every last savings account, CD, stock or bond, and the amount in each.

If you were a criminal, you would have the right to silence. But as a judgement debtor, you have no such right. And if you aren't truthful, you are committing perjury, a felony that can land you in prison for a long time. If you do attempt to transfer your assets after an accident or incident that creates liability, the court can invoke the fraudulent transfer laws and undo the transfer, cause forfeiture of other assets, impose heavy costs and punitive damages and even initiate criminal charges. You may think it is still your asset, but legally you now hold it in trust for the prospective claimant. The answer to this horrible nightmare is the offshore haven and the offshore Asset Protection Trust.

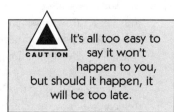
CAUTION It's all too easy to say it won't happen to you, but should it happen, it will be too late.

How offshore havens protect your assets

Offshore havens effectively protect assets in two principal ways. First, the offshore haven provides strict financial privacy and secrecy. If money is transferred correctly to an offshore haven, it will be exceptionally difficult for

U.S. creditors or litigants to locate. A U.S. creditor will be absolutely powerless to find out about your foreign accounts unless you disclose their existence.

While a judgment creditor can compel you to disclose your assets under oath, the use of offshore havens should not encourage perjury nor illegal concealment of your assets. You can have your money flow through intermediaries so that you can truthfully answer that you have no money because the offshore money is no longer yours. And you would not necessarily know where the funds are now located once the funds flow through intermediary accounts making it virtually impossible for claimants to link offshore assets to you or your companies.

The offshore haven does not provide asset protection, however, through its ability to keep your wealth a secret. You must assume that you will be compelled to disclose your offshore wealth under oath, or that your creditor will somehow discover your offshore holdings. Perhaps it will be through your tax returns. And even if you fail to report your offshore accounts to the IRS, your creditor may be more diligent than the IRS in discovering your violation. You will then not only be fighting the creditor but also the IRS.

Secrecy will keep less inquisitive creditors from your offshore assets, but if secrecy is not the chief asset protection mechanism, what is? Offshore havens chiefly protect assets because asset protection havens do not enforce foreign judgments or court orders. In most instances, the creditor would have to start a new lawsuit within the haven, and even this is usually futile.

> **note** From a practical standpoint, most cases can be tied up in litigation in America for over two years, thus leaving the creditor with no recourse offshore.

Starting litigation anew may fail for several reasons. The haven may not recognize the theory of liability on which the lawsuit is based. It may also be too late to start a fresh lawsuit because the haven may have a short statute of limitations or time period within which to sue. Some havens have only a two-year statute of limitations so lawsuits within these havens must commence within two years from the date of the claim, not two years from the date the funds were transferred offshore.

Even when the creditor must prove the assets were fraudulently transferred offshore, this is always difficult as most havens presume the debtor had no fraudulent intent when making the transfer. The havens used for asset protection have mitigated the Statute of Elizabeth on which fraudulent transfer claims are based. These are the Bahamas, the Caymans, the Cook Islands, Gibraltar, Turks and Caicos, Nevis, Belize, Cyprus and Mauritius. In each of these jurisdictions, a creditor's claim that assets were fraudulently transferred to an asset protection trust within the jurisdiction will fall largely on deaf ears.

Even when it is possible to sue offshore, it is usually prohibitively expensive and impractical in all but those relatively few cases that involve very large sums of money. Imagine the impracticality of prosecuting a lawsuit in the Cook Islands (in the South Pacific) or Gibraltar or Cyprus. This requires a most determined creditor.

HOT spot — Well-drafted offshore trusts contain a trigger provision that authorizes the trustee to transfer the trust assets to another jurisdiction should the trust come under attack.

Creditors who would chase offshore money through an offshore lawsuit still have little chance of recovery against an agile debtor who can continuously relocate his money to still other offshore havens until the creditor tires from the chase. Savvy investors deploy their assets among several havens so their creditors cannot conveniently grab their entire wealth to satisfy that one big claim. This creates a never-ending game of hopscotch designed to exhaust even the most determined creditor.

note

Thus, offshore asset protection plans are so designed that creditors cannot seize the offshore funds even if they do obtain an offshore judgment. Nor will offshore havens honor American judgments, IRS levies, subpoenas or summonses.

You can design your own offshore financial fortress. But, as with most asset protection strategies, offshore havens do not guarantee complete safety. The possibility always exists that a creditor can find and seize the offshore account. However, handled with even modest skill, offshore funds remain safe from all but the most clever, persistent, and luckiest creditor. Certainly, the creditor will need considerably more luck than if he chased your assets at home.

The asset protection trust

The primary offshore asset protection tool is aptly named the Asset Protection Trust, also commonly called the International Trust, Foreign-Based Trust or Creditor-Protection Trust.

Trusts date back to Roman and Greek law. Ancient Germanic and French law had similar legal arrangements, and the trust was a fundamental part of Islamic law. The trust was probably the world's first tax shelter: through feudal English trusts, citizens could avoid feudal taxes on property inheritances and transfers.

DEFINITION

A *trust* creates a legal relationship between three or more parties. The grantor or settlor creates the trust and usually funds it. The trustee takes legal title to the trust property and manages it according to the terms of the trust agreement and applicable trust law. The beneficiary receives money or property from the trust according to the trust terms.

For example, with many trusts you can be the grantor and create a trust and then name yourself the trustee as well as beneficiary. This often happens with the popular living trust used to avoid probate. When a trust is used to reduce or avoid taxes, the grantor, trustee and beneficiary are usually different parties. There often is more than one beneficiary but there is no legal limit on their number.

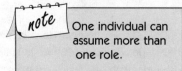

note

One individual can assume more than one role.

A trust can be revocable or irrevocable.

A revocable trust allows the grantor to abolish or alter the trust at any time. The grantor thus controls the trust assets, but this arrangement normally provides no tax benefits. An irrevocable trust permits the grantor few or no changes once the trust is created. An irrevocable trust is used for asset protection. Asset Protection Trusts may be either non-grantor or grantor trusts. The non-grantor trust provides asset protection and, possibly, income and estate tax benefits. The grantor trust is solely for asset protection and not for tax advantages.

With the non-grantor trust, the trust assets must go to your designated beneficiaries upon your death (and/or your spouse's death). It is therefore similar to the revocable living trust. Every non-grantor trust must:

• be irrevocable

• have non-citizens or non-residents of the U.S. as its trustees.

• prohibit distribution until after the death of the grantor and/or the grantor's spouse. (The grantor and the grantor's heirs, however, may receive loans or other advances on their bequests.)

Asset Protection Trusts are also written as Discretionary Trusts, which means the individual beneficiaries do not have vested interests. Instead, the trustee has wide discretion to invest the trust funds and distribute them to beneficiaries. The grantor becomes a contingent remainder beneficiary and

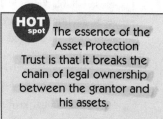

The essence of the Asset Protection Trust is that it breaks the chain of legal ownership between the grantor and his assets.

cannot have an immediate or direct beneficial interest in the trust. If the trustee has the discretion to distribute trust assets, the reversionary interest of the grantor must be contingent upon the trustee not exercising this power. This discretionary power in the trustee renders the reversionary interest nonvested. Creditors who then attempt to attach this reversionary interest would unsuccessfully seek to elevate their rights above those of the named beneficiaries. Since the reversionary interest has no value—because it can be destroyed by distributing the principal at the trustee's discretion—the creditor cannot reach that reversionary interest.

Asset Protection Trusts must also have at least one more beneficiary when the debtor is a beneficiary. Courts have held that in a sole beneficiary trust, the beneficiary can terminate the trust and, therefore, the debtor's creditors have that same right.

DEFINITION

The hallmark of the discretionary *Asset Protection Trust* is that the beneficiaries, in point of law, have no vested interest in the trust property, indeed no quantifiable interest at all, having only an expectancy or the possibility of an interest that is not the least susceptible to capture by a judgment creditor nor transmittable to a trustee-in-bankruptcy.

Where the grantor is to be a beneficiary, the greatest care should be taken to ensure that he is not expressed to be the sole beneficiary of income. The basis of this caution is that a trustee's discretionary power to pay or not to pay income to a sole beneficiary has been held to determine upon the bankruptcy of such beneficiary with the right to income thereupon vesting in his trustee-in-bankruptcy. In this instance, the exercise by the trustee of a power to accumulate could save the day. Otherwise, since the sole beneficiary in such a case is entitled to terminate the trust in his favor and to demand payment of the whole fund, these rights will pass automatically to his trustee-in-bankruptcy.

note

A trustee-in-bankruptcy is powerless to reach the bankrupt's interest where the bankrupt is but one of the beneficiaries under a true discretionary trust. This is so because the trustees of such a settlement would be under no obligation to distribute.

Thus, if the trustees, in the exercise of their fiduciary discretion decide to exclude a particular beneficiary from an otherwise general distribution, or alternatively, to exercise their power of accumulation so as to make no distribution at all, there is nothing a bankruptcy trustee or judgment creditor could do to make it otherwise.

HOT spot An Asset Protection Trust should always be a true discretionary trust involving two or more discretionary beneficiaries.

If the grantor has the power to revoke the trust, upon his bankruptcy this right will go to his bankruptcy trustee who may then collapse the trust for the benefit of the grantor's creditors, subject, of course, to any vested rights of other beneficiaries under the trust. Therefore, the retention by the grantor of a power of revocation is perilous and has no place in an Asset Protection Trust. The grantor, may, however, reserve a limited power of appointment under which he appoints the trust assets to a designated class.

note The irrevocability of the trust is also critical in its structuring.

All this leads to several important questions.

1) Who should be the beneficiaries?

2) Who should be the trustee?

3) How do you protect the funds entrusted to the trustee and how do you control the trust's investment decisions?

4) How do you repatriate your funds?

The first question, the chain of beneficiaries, has already been covered. You can be a beneficiary provided you have at least one additional beneficiary. Most often, other family members are named as beneficiaries. It is also common to name a charity, such as the American Red Cross, so as to leave the family undisclosed. The grantor, through a side letter of wishes, then designates the family members as the true beneficiaries.

Who should be the trustee? You can initially serve as a co-trustee and resign when you are in financial danger. This gives you direct control until it is no longer safe to remain a

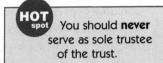

HOT *spot* You should **never** serve as sole trustee of the trust.

trustee. You want a trustee who is not a U.S. citizen or resident and, therefore, is not subject to the jurisdiction of U.S. courts. This may be a foreign bank, trust company or a professional who customarily serves in that capacity. Foreign trustees are very trustworthy and accommodating. Their fees can vary considerably, depending upon who they are, their haven and the amount in trust. Typically, fees range between $500 and $4,000 a year.

How do you protect the funds entrusted to the trustee? Of course, there is no substitute for diligence in choosing a trustworthy trustee. A bank as trustee should certainly allay any fears.

You can also have the trust contain protective language that lets you replace the trustee whenever you wish. This ensures that the trustee will manage the trust as you instruct. But it can be dangerous if you have too much control over the trustee and, hence, the trust. At the most, your trust should only set parameters for a trustee—such as "a bank in the trust jurisdiction, with assets over $10 million, and in which the grantor holds less than three percent ownership."

How do you control the trustee and his investment policies? The trust may provide for a committee of advisors or protectors to advise the trustee regarding investments and trust administration. As committee chair, the grantor can retain indirect control of the trust. The trustees, however, must be free to ignore the committee's advice and thus avoid the argument that the committee has legal control over the trust. To protect against a trustee who unsatisfactorily performs his trust duties, the committee can have the power to remove and replace the trustee. The committee should also have the power to add or delete a class of beneficiaries to help protect against such unforeseen circumstances as divorce or uncooperative beneficiaries.

The protector may also have the power to veto the trustee's decisions, however, such a protector should reside outside the United States and not within U.S. court jurisdiction.

Additionally, the trust should recite limitations on the trustee's authority. The right to change trustees is another vital control. Most important is that your proposed trustee understand your investment objectives and restrictions. Offshore trustees generally allow the grantor to dictate investment policy. Therefore, in practice, you retain virtually the same control over your offshore funds as if they were in your name onshore.

The last question is how you reclaim your money once you shelter it in a trust. Generally, once a creditor sees there are no assets to easily seize, the debtor can settle the affair quite cheaply. Alternatively, the debtor can go bankrupt on the claim. The funds, if correctly transferred to the offshore trust, will be safe from U.S. creditors and the bankruptcy trustee. In either instance, the funds can then be repatriated to the U.S. There is an important caution: offshore funds are not protected from foreign creditors under a U.S. bankruptcy. So it's important that your offshore entities remain creditor-free.

Offshore funds may also be freely distributed to the beneficiaries of the trust, if the trust gives the trustee broad discretionary powers, as is typically the case. Even a sizeable estate can be distributed to family members who may then repatriate the funds to the U.S.

It is not uncommon to find an Asset Protection Trust owning foreign companies that are alter egos of the debtor. The trust funds may then flow back through these companies to the U.S. through layered transactions.

The debtor should hold no officerships or directorships in these trust-owned offshore companies. They are ordinarily managed by "straws" on behalf of the debtor, usually friends, relatives or other offshore professionals who are readily available to serve in these capacities.

The most direct way to repatriate your money is simply to borrow whatever funds you need from the trust. You can borrow from your trust, and therefore you never lose access to your funds. Of course, your repatriated funds must still be protected from creditors. The easiest way to accomplish this is to assign the loan proceeds to a spouse's account or set up a corporation to receive the funds.

How to shelter your assets offshore

Generally, liquid and portable assets are held in the Asset Protection Trust: cash, securities and collectibles—such as gold or jewelry. It serves no purpose to title your real estate or other mainland possessions—such as mainland securities—to the trust because they remain within the jurisdiction of the U.S. courts, just as the trustees and protectors must be non-residents and non-citizens of the U.S. so they also remain beyond the reach of the American courts.

> **HOT spot** To be protected, the asset must be physically outside the United States.

For this reason, all U.S. investments are converted to foreign investments. We usually recommend Swiss Plus annuities, or quality mutual funds, such as the Templeton Funds, Scudders or T. Rowe. There are, however, many others.

The point is that any U.S.-based trust asset is subject to attack by U.S. creditors, notwithstanding their trust ownership.

You may prefer not to heavily fund the trust until it is absolutely necessary. Most people wish to keep their assets onshore, in their current investments, until seriously threatened. The Asset Protection Trust accommodates this. One way is to have the trust become a limited partner in a U.S. limited partnership. The debtor would be a general partner who decides whether and when his assets are transferred to the trust.

The partnership assets never need be distributed to the Asset Protection Trust nor leave the United States unless absolutely necessary. The United States assets may also be wired to an offshore International Business Corporation as an intermediary—to add a layer of confidentiality to the trust.

In practice, the partnership funds at risk would stay in the partnership account at a local bank. If attacked by creditors under a fraudulent transfer claim, the partnership would distribute the funds to the Asset Protection Trust as its major limited partner. The funds would then be wired offshore to the trust—possibly through the intermediary company.

You cannot use an Asset Protection Trust to protect real estate or other tangible mainland possessions, but you can sell or mortgage the asset so no equity remains exposed to creditors. The sale or loan proceeds are then sent offshore to the trust. The objective is to leave no asset with equity exposed in the United States.

You cannot give a U.S. court the power to aid a creditor hoping to seize your assets. With the trust assets physically outside the U.S., they are beyond U.S. court authority. With a foreign trustee in control of the trust, a U.S. court cannot hold you in contempt if you fail to obey an order to repatriate the funds. This is because you cannot do that which is beyond your legal power.

> **HOT spot** A U.S. judge cannot compel you to return the assets to the U.S., if you are not a trustee or protector.

How to build stronger protection

The Asset Protection Trust is versatile. It can do more than safely shelter offshore wealth. Used creatively, it can build protection for you and your family in several different ways:

- The Asset Protection Trust can loan you back your own money and to secure repayment, encumber your mainland assets. The repayment terms can be so unattractive that creditors would not pursue the pledged asset. Because you indirectly control the trust, you can modify the terms of payment or security, while the trust as lienholder can claim your mainland assets ahead of other creditors.

- Similarly, you can borrow money from the trust with a shared appreciation mortgage. This allows you to borrow money from the trust while you agree to repay the loan at a lower interest rate in exchange for the trust receiving a share of the property's appreciation. This is common with offshore trusts. The part of the profits that eventually goes to the trust is tax deductible by you, and tax deferred until your death by the trust. This arrangement quickly diffuses creditors.

- Do you own a business with receivables? You can sell the receivables to your trust at a discount. This has several advantages. One advantage is that the difference between the discounted purchase price and the payments received by the trust can be tax deferred until your death. You can also warrant that the receivables sold to the trust are fully collectible. To guarantee this, you can encumber your mainland assets to the trust. This gives you long-term tax deferral and asset protection!

- You may also transfer assets to the trust in exchange for a private annuity. A private annuity is an agreement by the trust to pay you and/or your spouse a fixed future income that continues until your death. This private annuity has many advantages: First, the assets transferred to the Asset Protection Trust for the private annuity are now beyond creditor reach. Second, any assets transferred to the trust reduce your estate by their value. Third, you can transfer appreciated assets to the trust so the property can be sold by the trust on a tax-deferred basis.

Tax implications of the asset protection trust

 Foreign asset protection trusts are tax-neutral and are usually treated the same as domestic trusts. This means income from the trust is treated and taxed as the grantor's personal income. Because the grantor retains control over the transfer of assets to the foreign trust, U.S. gift taxes can usually be avoided. But that degree of control can make the grantor vulnerable to court orders requiring the grantor to exercise that control, thus defeating the asset protection benefits.

Estate taxes are imposed on the grantor's estate for the value of the trust assets, but existing exemptions—such as those for marital assets -can still be used. Asset Protection Trusts are not subject to the 35 percent US. excise tax imposed on transfers of property to a foreign person.

Because Asset Protection Trusts are usually tax-neutral, there is little IRS scrutiny. Depending upon the trust's structure, there may be some minor disclosure requirements, but these are neither burdensome nor destroy privacy.

 It is sometimes possible to combine an Asset Protection Trust with a foreign business, or investment, to reduce or eliminate U.S. income taxes. The alternatives and opportunities here are as varied as the imaginable arrangements. Tax-wise, this can become extremely complicated, as it frequently involves controlled foreign corporations, foreign personal holding companies, foreign sales companies, passive foreign investment companies and other "daisy-chain" entities that collectively allow you to legally escape taxes. The tax advantages of offshore Asset Protection Trusts can be staggering.

There is one additional benefit—and drawback—to the offshore trust. The benefit is that like a living trust, the trust lets you avoid probate and its red tape, delay and expense. It does not help you avoid estate taxes, which ensnare all U.S. citizens—regardless of where their wealth is.

The drawback? Assets placed in trust, and any proceeds not needed for the support or education of the beneficiary, are subject to U.S. gift taxes.

Maximize asset protection with your own bank

> Operating your own offshore bank significantly adds asset protection. I recommend offshore bank ownership for offshore funds over $500,000, or to stymie a particularly zealous creditor.

Owning your own offshore bank is an extremely effective way to add privacy to an Asset Protection Trust or offshore company. The offshore bank insulates because it makes it extremely difficult for creditors to identify assets deposited to the bank's general fund. Once those assets are invested, it becomes impossible to link those assets to the property or collateral obtained in exchange. Offshore banks are expected to widely invest their assets. Individuals are not. A bank's broad investment powers thus cloak the movement of assets without drawing attention or suspicion.

An offshore bank's privacy feature can also help you if, for instance, you become immersed in a major business lawsuit and your opponent subpoenas sensitive financial information or trade secrets. Store these records in your own offshore bank, and they will be protected from U.S. court orders and subpoenas.

To patent an idea in the U.S., you must disclose it to the U.S. Patent Office and the prying eyes of inquisitive competitors who, with minor modifications, can exploit your

> Owning an offshore bank is also the best way to protect your ideas.

idea before you even gain a foothold on the market. It is smarter to apply for a patent through your private offshore bank, where the "idea" would be financial information protected under the haven's bank secrecy laws.

Offshore protection against product liability claims

Companies that conduct their business through offshore companies, as well as banks, also gain asset protection because they have immunity against American-based product liability claims. For example, as a manufacturer of a defective product within the U.S., you would be liable to those injured through the use of your product.

If you manufactured the product through an offshore company, you would have no liability because your manufacturing company did not directly do business within the U.S. The plaintiff could sue the U.S. distributor, but this would be of little consequence if the U.S. distributor had few or no assets. This U.S. distributor may even be a "shell" subsidiary of your foreign manufacturing company. As you can see, an international organization may be your safest organization.

Protection from the IRS

The greatest number of offshore exiles are doctors attempting to protect their wealth from malpractice claims. The next largest group are taxpayers besieged by the IRS.

Mortal creditors and litigants can usually be stonewalled by standard domestic asset protection shelters—such as state homestead laws, exemption statutes and limited partnerships. But the IRS is not so easily discouraged. A taxpayer's assets may be unsafe from IRS seizure unless sheltered offshore because many of the laws that do safeguard assets against creditor claims are not effective against the IRS.

Offshore havens do not generally enforce an IRS levy, summons or other IRS attempts to discover or seize assets. But some havens, such as Switzerland, have been known to routinely enforce IRS seizures. Offshore banks with U.S. branches are also too friendly with the IRS to be valuable as asset protectors.

Taxpayers chased by the IRS usually sell or mortgage their assets to liquidate their wealth which is then moved offshore. And this even works against the IRS if the offshore transfer can be completed before the tax lien is filed.

The IRS won't quickly compromise your tax liability once it sees you've hidden your money offshore, but it may suspend collection and stop the chase once it realizes that further efforts to seize your assets will be futile.

Asset protection using Swiss annuities

Another popular way to utilize the laws of the offshore havens to protect your wealth is to buy Swiss annuities.

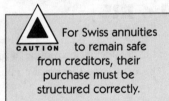

For Swiss annuities to remain safe from creditors, their purchase must be structured correctly.

Under Swiss law, insurance policies, including annuities, cannot be seized by creditors or a trustee-in-bankruptcy. Swiss authorities will not allow the seizure, even if it has been ordered by an American court.

The first requirement is that an American who purchases a Swiss annuity must designate his or her spouse as beneficiary. A third party may be named irrevocably. Second, the individual must have purchased the annuity or designated the beneficiaries at least six months prior to a lawsuit or a bankruptcy.

The annuity can also be protected by converting a designation of children or spouse as beneficiary into an irrevocable designation when the annuity appears endangered.

Swiss law states that if a policy holder designates a spouse or children as beneficiaries, those beneficiaries then become policy holders and the original policy holder automatically loses all rights under the policy. This, of course, would also extend to his creditors. And it does not matter whether the designation is revocable or irrevocable. The policy holder may revocably designate his spouse or children as beneficiary and revoke this before the annuity expires, assuming there is no further creditor threat.

Swiss annuities are not only exceptional asset protectors, but they also are safer than U.S. annuities. Swiss annuities are regulated to insure adequate funding. They denominate accounts in the strong Swiss franc and the annuity payout is guaranteed. Swiss annuities are also exempt from the 35 percent withholding tax levied on foreign bank accounts, and Swiss annuities are not reportable to the IRS or Swiss tax agents.

I recommend Swiss Plus annuities, but there are other excellent annuities. Conversion of your vulnerable American cash and investments to Swiss annuities may be the easiest and fastest way to gain solid asset protection.

Combine asset protection strategies

Seldom can you put all your assets offshore. You must then combine domestic asset protection tactics with your offshore protection strategies.

If tangible assets are titled to an offshore trust or company, a U.S. court can determine that these assets were titled offshore to defraud creditors and can undo the transfer since U.S. courts retain jurisdiction over property within the U.S., regardless of how

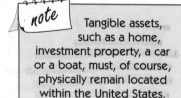

note Tangible assets, such as a home, investment property, a car or a boat, must, of course, physically remain located within the United States.

titled. Last-minute transfers of these assets then leave them vulnerable.

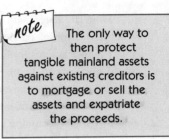

The only way to then protect tangible mainland assets against existing creditors is to mortgage or sell the assets and expatriate the proceeds.

If you do not presently have claims against you but want protection for the future, you have several onshore asset protection options:

- State homestead laws may protect your home.

- You may convert your unprotected investments into exempt assets—such as annuities or insurance that are protected in many states from creditors.

- You and your spouse may title assets as tenants-by-the-entirety, which in some states also offers protection against creditors of one spouse.

- Corporations may hold certain assets safe from creditors. Nevada and Wyoming corporations, for example, offer a level of secrecy protection that compares to the offshore havens.

- Domestic trusts—particularly the irrevocable trust—can safely hold assets.

Revocable living trusts provide no asset protection.

- You may mortgage your property to a "friendly" creditor, and thus leave no equity for less friendly creditors.

- You may set up a family limited partnership which have become enormously popular for asset protection. Family limited partnerships allow you to retain maximum control over the partnership assets while providing considerable protection against creditors.

How does a limited partnership work? The partnership usually owns most of the family assets (except for the family home, pensions and IRAs). The husband and wife may be the general partners and thus control the assets. The husband, as the at-risk spouse, may own only one percent of the partnership. His creditors would then be entitled to only one percent of the distributed profits or one percent of the partnership proceeds—when the partnership is liquidated. Since creditors could gain nothing more, they would have no reasonable prospects of recovery.

The remaining 99 percent of the partnership may be owned by other family members, or various trusts, such as a children's trust. An offshore Asset Protection Trust can also be a major limited partner.

A combination limited partnership and Asset Protection Trust can be a smart strategy if you have been hit with a major lawsuit. On one hand, you may not want your funds offshore if the lawsuit can be resolved. On the other hand, you cannot leave your assets exposed in case you lose the case. You would then keep your assets in the partnership until they are in clear danger (probably just before trial). The assets would then be liquidated (through sale or refinancing) and distributed to the partners. The offshore Asset Protection Trust as a major partner would receive a major share of the proceeds, which would be placed offshore beyond creditor reach.

There are variations on the theme. Some domestic offshore-asset protection arrangements are quite elaborate. And unlike the Asset Protection Trust alone, a combination of trust, limited partnership and a privately owned offshore bank that serves as trustee, can create a mighty formidable financial fortress.

The key is to keep your money flowing between various domestic and offshore entities so it becomes impossible for a creditor to trace or reach.

These asset protection strategies must be customized to the individual case and take into consideration many factors: the nature and value of the assets, the financial threat, the family structure, tax and estate planning considerations, and other asset protection alternatives.

Do you want to learn more about asset protection? Read my best-selling book: *Asset Protection Secrets* (available from Garrett Publishing). This book reveals 234 asset protection strategies that can protect everything you own from lawsuits, creditors, the IRS or divorce. It details how a Family Limited Partnership-Asset Protection Trust combination can shelter your assets and help you build a financial fortress that ensures your lifelong security.

Key points to remember

◆ In today's America, your assets are highly vulnerable to lawsuits, creditors, the IRS, divorce and various other dangers. Offshore havens can provide safety for your wealth.

◆ Offshore havens protect assets from all U.S. court judgments, orders, and subpoenas. You do not "hide" your assets offshore—you protect them.

◆ The Asset Protection Trust is the primary tool to gain offshore protection. To be effective, however, it must be properly structured.

◆ Owning your own offshore bank can increase your offshore protection.

◆ Swiss annuities are generally safe from American creditors—and are excellent investments.

◆ For maximum asset protection, combine your offshore strategies with your domestic creditor-proofing arrangements.

The artful use of tax havens

6

Chapter 6

The artful use
of tax havens

DEFINITION

Evasion is the illegal and the willful criminal attempt to violate U.S. tax laws. This includes the failure to declare income earned offshore. In general, U.S. residents must declare and pay income taxes on income earned anywhere in the world. This includes income earned offshore.

note

Tax havens significantly reduce, defer or even totally eliminate all taxes. You can accomplish this either through tax evasion or tax avoidance.

CAUTION

Offshore ventures and banking do present enormous opportunities to illegally evade taxes. This is because offshore banks and businesses do not issue 1099 forms to the IRS or other informational reports about your offshore earnings. Only you know what you earn offshore, so you are strictly on the honor system when your money is making you more money overseas.

Who knows how many overseas investors fail to declare their overseas income? The number is undoubtedly staggering. While there is a clear opportunity to evade taxes offshore, exploring these techniques is not my objective.

Instead, I want to show you how to avoid taxes legally by taking advantage of the many little-known U.S. tax laws that provide perfectly legitimate tax reduction opportunities for savvy tax haven investors. In summary, I want you to master the art of offshore tax avoidance.

The end to tax tyranny?

One elderly couple recently griped to me that over half their income goes to taxes. When they die, Uncle Sam will grab half, again, of what they've scrimped a lifetime to save. They had reason to gripe. Fortunately, I had some good news for them. Since most of their income came from investments, they could, through the artful use of tax havens, legally escape the confiscatory taxes destined to obliterate their wealth.

> **note** The exploding interest in tax havens is chiefly because more and more Americans, as well as nationals from other major countries, are tax oppressed.

Of course, neither confiscatory taxes nor taxpayer maneuvers to avoid these taxes are new. Ancient governments adroitly plundered wealth from their citizenry and their taxpayers also rebelled, revolted or started wars in protest. Luckily, today we have another option: journey to a less tax-voracious land, one we call a tax haven.

The tax-oppressed find tax havens a most convenient way to legally avoid taxes. They quickly discover that by relocating their wealth offshore, they can keep most, if not all, of it and thus build wealth much faster than if they invested at home—where it would be subject to the tax-bite.

> **note** Our best tax specialists cannot comprehend today's tax laws. Planning is out.

The tax-bite is only one reason to escape the U.S. tax system. Uncertainty is another. U.S. tax laws, while always complex, are more bewildering with each passing year. We never know what our tax bill will be until it is too late. Not only are our tax laws becoming increasingly complex, they are also less equitable because taxes finance our runaway spending. Americans protest about how much they are forced to pay in taxes and protest even more about how our taxes are spent. Americans are tired of funding a welfare state, and bailing out foreign countries. Most of all, Americans are tired of waste and corruption in government. The net effect is that most Americans are no longer wed to the idea that paying taxes is patriotic. That's why Americans are moving their money offshore.

U.S. taxes have an extraordinarily long reach. They touch virtually all people and all transactions. Taxes are especially difficult to escape in the United States because citizens of the U.S. and the Philippines are taxed on their worldwide income. Other countries generally tax their citizens to their water's edge.

Only when you compare the magnitude and complexity of the U.S. tax system can you appreciate the liberality and simplicity of the tax laws in offshore havens—and why they are your best escape route from runaway taxes.

Offshore tax planning is not everyone's panacea. I can barely begin to fully cover every situation or intricacy. But this chapter will give you a broad picture of what may be possible, so read carefully!

If you have substantial assets or taxable earnings and want tax

> **note** Offshore tax planning requires a consummate knowledge of U.S. tax law, the tax laws of the haven, and how to legally and effectively mesh the two tax laws to your optimum advantage.

> ⚠️ **CAUTION** Tax specialists seldom agree on tax strategies, so taxpayers must often choose between conflicting opinions.

avoidance, then you must consult a good tax specialist, one thoroughly familiar with international tax planning and well-experienced with your haven's tax laws. Expect differences of opinion between your tax advisors about what will be your best strategy.

International tax strategies artfully exploit the numerous loopholes in the tax laws, and there are plenty of loopholes to be found offshore. So utilize a loophole or two in our tax laws, until Congress gets around to closing them.

Avoiding U.S. taxes through offshore investing requires aggressive planning, and a willingness, even enthusiasm, to exploit oversights in our tax laws. To stand on firm legal ground while enjoying substantial tax savings abroad is the ultimate aphrodisiac at tax time.

Just as there are endless offshore tax-avoidance loopholes, for the same reason the IRS cannot conceivably close them all. And for each loophole closed by the IRS, another one or two are discovered. Offshore tax planning is a game of chess.

How tax havens save taxes

DEFINITION

What is a tax haven? *Tax havens* are offshore havens with low taxes or no taxes; certainly far lower taxes than those of your own country.

Nationals from every country exploit tax havens. Most coined a phrase for these havens. Germans refer to it as *eine steuroase*—or a tax oasis. To the French, it is *un paradise fiscal*—or a tax paradise. These names are accurate because a good tax haven is both an oasis from oppressive taxation and thus a paradise. A land without taxes may be the closest we will ever come to a true paradise!

Tax havens are everywhere, and of every size and political persuasion. Many, but not all, are tiny, scenic Caribbean islands. Hong Kong is a prime tax haven because it gives huge tax breaks to foreign-source income. Austria and Switzerland are popular tax havens. They do this for a wide variety of self-serving reasons, but mostly to attract industry to stimulate their economy.

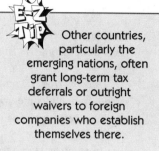

E-Z TIP — Other countries, particularly the emerging nations, often grant long-term tax deferrals or outright waivers to foreign companies who establish themselves there.

Although difficult to imagine, if you are a foreigner and bank or invest with U.S. financial institutions, you may consider America a tax haven. This is because America does not tax foreigners on U.S.-earned income. Conversely, a foreign haven may tax an American's income earned within the haven, although the tax is usually minimal.

So any country can be considered a tax haven, because every country taxes certain transactions more leniently than do other countries. Each country, therefore, attracts capital for its tax-privileged transactions.

What we consider a tax haven may be regarded as a tax tyranny by its own residents, because most tax havens have dual taxation, or a two-tiered tax structure: They impose higher taxes on resident income than on non-residents. Outside investment income usually incurs little or no tax, which is how the tax haven gets its name.

Large, industrialized, high-tax nations tolerate the tax havens that siphon much of their income because their own huge multinational corporations obtain much of their income from these havens, particularly those that are also banking centers. This is the trade-off, and one reason tax havens have grown economically to become major players in the world's capital markets.

To better understand international tax strategy, you must understand how the different types of income are taxed. Essentially, there are two types of income: From labor and from invested capital.

DEFINITION

Income from labor includes salaries, bonuses, commissions and professional fees. The tax havens do not provide much opportunity to reduce taxes from income on labor.

DEFINITION

Income from capital includes earnings from investments: stocks, bonds, savings, rental income, royalties or loans. It is here that the tax haven excels and can offer Americans significant tax savings.

In summary, tax havens are designed to shelter investment income and profits, not wages. But there are still ways to shelter wages earned overseas, as you will see later in this chapter.

The joys of a tax-free business

Tax havens were true tax havens before 1962. Then you could simply set up an offshore corporation, divert your income to the corporation, and defer all U.S. taxes on the income until it was repatriated to the U.S. If you transacted business between your mainland company and offshore company, you could keep your U.S. company unprofitable and untaxed while you accumulated tax-free profits offshore. That has changed.

As I already pointed out, America may be your best tax haven—if you are not an American. In fact, most Americans are surprised to learn that the United States is considered an attractive tax haven by foreign investors. While U.S. citizens pay hefty federal, state and local taxes, foreign investors can invest virtually tax free in the United States.

U.S. tax laws and tax treaties, when understood and manipulated, provide excellent opportunities for foreign investors who seek low- or no-tax U.S. investments. In fact, U.S. tax lawyers and accountants who target inbound capital and structure U.S.

The United States is not a typical no-tax haven like the Caymans or Bahamas.

transactions for foreign investors are busier than ever.

Like most offshore havens, the United States encourages tax- free foreign investment because we need foreign capital to finance the economy and our ever-growing budget deficit. I expect America to more aggressively pursue foreign funds as our deficit grows.

As Americans do when they invest offshore, foreigners benefit chiefly by combining the U.S. tax laws with their own. While the United States taxes its citizens and residents on their worldwide income; non-citizens and non-residents are not taxed on certain income earned in the U.S. Foreigners who invest in the United States exploit these non-taxable situations.

Under the right circumstances, American citizens and residents can benefit from these same laws that allow foreigners tax-free income from U.S. investments. As an American, you can establish your own offshore corporation to invest tax-free or tax-deferred in U.S. or global investments.

The offshore corporate loophole

First you must understand the offshore corporate loophole. Before 1962, you could set up an offshore corporation and have it invest tax free. If the corporation had no U.S. address, it was considered a non-resident foreign corporation and it could earn tax-free income until it actually distributed dividends. Dividends then paid to U.S. shareholders would, of course, then be taxable.

Since U.S. shareholders in such a foreign corporation are taxed as partners in a partnership, they pay an apportioned share of the income of the foreign corporation as it is earned—even if the profit is retained by the corporation and not paid out to the stockholders in dividends. This change in tax law initially killed the incentive behind the tax haven corporation. Fortunately, two other tax loopholes came to the rescue that still allow Americans tax-free investments through their own offshore corporations.

The "decontrol" loophole

DEFINITION

A U.S. shareholder of an offshore corporation is taxed on its annual income—but only if it is considered a *Controlled Foreign Corporation (CFC)*. An offshore corporation is a CFC if more than 50 percent of its voting power is owned or controlled by Americans. But you can organize an offshore corporation so that it is not a CFC.

But it is not as easy to accomplish as you may think. First, understand what will not work. You cannot hire a tax haven lawyer, accountant or a professional director to be your "straw" and hold 50 percent or more of the corporate stock so it appears the corporation is decontrolled when it legally and functionally remains under your control. These sham arrangements are treated as though you owned all the stock, and will result in your corporation being classified as a CFC.

The IRS is also wise to daisy chain arrangements of trusts and corporations that own the stock of the U.S. investor corporation. These daisy-chain arrangements may be challenged, and the IRS and courts look beyond the "chain," and can conclude that since you set up the chain, you constructively own or control a CFC. The upside is that the IRS does not easily uncover these arrangements, nor does it always win its challenges.

DEFINITION

How can you legally decontrol an offshore corporation? Start by defining a U.S. person. A *U.S. person* is any U.S. citizen or resident who owns 10 percent or more of the offshore corporation's voting stock. So one obvious way to decontrol a foreign corporation is to have no U.S. citizen or resident own 10 percent or more of the corporation. For instance, if you and at least 10 associates equally own the offshore corporation, it will qualify as a decontrolled offshore corporation because no one U.S. citizen or resident owns 10 percent or more of its voting stock. The company, like resident aliens, can then invest in the United States or elsewhere with no immediate tax consequences to its shareholders, and the income can compound tax free in the corporation.

You must also observe the attribution of ownership rule which provides that if related U.S. taxpayers are shareholders, they will be considered to collectively own the shares for purposes of determining control. For example, if two or more family members each own 10 percent of the shares, the corporation will be considered a CFC. Similarly, if you own several U.S. corporations that are shareholders of a foreign company, they will be considered one, not separate shareholders, and you will again have a CFC.

If one U.S. resident owns 50 percent or more of the voting stock, and other U.S. residents each own less than 10 percent of the voting shares, a CFC is also created because more than 50 percent is controlled by U.S. shareholders. But here, only the 50 percent shareholder is taxed by the US. on his pro -rata share of the corporation's earned income. The others are not "U.S. shareholders" because each owns less than 10 percent and is thus taxed as a stockholder in a decontrolled corporation.

Another strategy to decontrol an offshore corporation is to invest with one or more unrelated foreign partners who own 50 percent or more of the voting shares. If the corporation then invests in the United States as a non-resident alien, you are taxed only on the dividends you receive.

CAUTION
The foreign participants must be bona-fide investors and true owners of the stock, not simply your agents or "straws."

The above arrangement is particularly popular among foreign investors from countries with similar tax rules. For example, American and German investors often co-invest in U.S. real estate, and both correctly declare to their respective taxing authorities that they are not in control of their corporation.

The favored income loophole

You can possibly avoid U.S. taxes even if you completely control an offshore CFC. This is because U.S. shareholders are taxed only on certain earned income from a CFC: Subpart F income. All other income is taxed as if the corporation were decontrolled. Income, therefore, accumulates tax free in the corporation until it is distributed.

DEFINITION

Subpart F income includes interest, dividends, royalties, gains on securities, plus rents from related parties. So most investment profits are considered Subpart F income. But rent or income from actively conducting a trade or business is not Subpart F income unless it is received from a related party.

For instance, if you lease rental units in the Bahamas to unrelated parties, this would be considered a rental trade or business in a foreign country, and the rental income would not be Subpart F income.

Consulting services, such as management, architectural or engineering, performed for an unrelated person are not subpart F income and can accumulate tax-free offshore.

There are other Subpart F incomes, as well as special rules for banking, insurance, shipping and oil service incomes, which are earned overseas and probably can avoid the Subpart F rules. There are many other loopholes to Subpart F income.

Avoid the investment company trap

In a valiant effort to close the offshore corporation loopholes, the 1986 Tax Reform Act introduced tough passive- foreign-investment-company (PFIC) rules.

A *PFIC* is any foreign corporation with:

1) 75 percent or more of its gross income as passive income, or

2) at least 50 percent of the value of its assets producing passive income (or held for the production of passive income), which includes interest, dividends, capital gains, royalties and certain other incomes.

Unlike a CFC, the PFIC has no control requirement. An offshore corporation with a one percent American ownership, but with this minimum passive income, is nevertheless a PFIC.

Several tax penalties arise for owning PFIC shares, and they are payable when you either sell your shares or take an excess distribution. (The penalty tax assumes that the undistributed income and gains of the PFIC were distributed annually.) You must pay the tax plus interest for every year you held the shares without payment.

The PFIC can instead elect to become a "qualified electing corporation," which reports income and gains annually, as do U.S.-based mutual funds. You, of course, then lose the big benefit of tax deferring your income, which is a prime reason for offshore investing.

To avoid the PFIC penalty you can either reduce the offshore corporation's passive income or combine the offshore corporation's investments with an offshore business—such as offshore manufacturing.

Investment loopholes in the United States

As you can see, a correctly structured offshore corporation can invest tax free in the United States, or at least with minimum tax consequences if the offshore corporation remains a foreign corporation not engaged in a U.S. trade under U.S. tax law.

To avoid tax problems, become a student of the many IRS regulations and rules. Most important, have your business maintain no U.S. office or resident agent. Keep its books and records offshore. Have a competent U.S. tax advisor structure your business affairs to fully comply with the tax laws.

Your offshore corporation will give you some big benefits: you'll pay no U.S. taxes on bank-deposit interest nor capital gains earned on U.S. stocks and bonds. Even taxed dividends from U.S. stocks can often become tax free if you choose a haven with a favorable tax treaty with the United States, and this can significantly lower your dividend withholding tax rate.

U.S. real estate investments were historically the chosen path to tax-free income and gains for non-resident aliens. Since 1980, these profits are also no longer tax-free. But, a decontrolled offshore corporation can still have lower taxable profits if the transaction follows complicated and rapidly changing laws, which usually involves an offshore company in a haven with a favorable U.S. tax treaty. The offshore company may establish a U.S. company to buy the real estate, and another to manage the property for management fees.

With some planning, any U.S. citizen or resident can take advantage of one or more offshore corporations for tax-free investing. But taking advantage of these loopholes requires detailed knowledge of U.S. tax laws, which goes beyond these few broad-brush possibilities.

> **HINT** Updated revenue rulings do challenge these and similar tax-maneuvers, so a constant review of your organization and its practices by a U.S. tax advisor is essential.

Safe offshore investing also means avoiding the various schemes, such as the "daisy chain" where linked foreign corporations and trusts are in fact controlled by Americans. Also avoid foreign lawyers and agents who claim that if they take "control" of your entity you will be safe from the IRS. Also beware of plans that use secrecy as the path to escape taxes. Hiding offshore is not the right strategy. Finally, don't set up a "thinly capitalized" foreign corporation with few or no assets.

Many Americans could and would take advantage of the offshore corporation tax loophole if they knew about it. Operating your own offshore corporation—with zero or low taxes—is a terrific way to do business and build wealth without it being confiscated by Uncle Sam.

There's a tax haven for every business

CAUTION Tax havens cannot solve every tax problem. You must select a tax haven that fits your needs, objectives and requirements.

Tax havens have grown in popularity with the multi-national company that are frequently headquartered in a tax haven with shareholders from many different countries. This insures no one country completely controls the corporation.

Companies pick and choose tax havens to save taxes. But what saves a company taxes in one instance may not save taxes for another company, in another industry, presented with an entirely different set of circumstances. Some examples:

- Tax laws in both the United States and Great Britain offer tax savings for mutual funds located in tax havens. International investment companies can advantageously invest in Britain and the United States because both British and American restrictions regarding the time a security must be held to qualify for the lower capital gains tax rate does not apply to tax haven companies. So mutual funds and investment trusts can be set up in tax havens, and investors worldwide avoid the usual taxes on these investments.

- Favorable ship registration laws draw shipping companies to Panama and Liberia. However, Greece, the Bahamas, Bermuda, Hong Kong, Cyprus, Malta and other nations entice shippers from Panama

141

and Liberia with still other inducements. Greece, for example, relaxes customs duties, vehicle registration fees and income tax. So shipping companies gain tax advantages by incorporating in Panama or Liberia, while keeping their headquarters in Greece. Few countries tax the income of foreign shipping companies, so a tax haven is particularly advantageous to shippers.

• Manufacturers who depend upon transportation or skilled labor will not find the typical tax haven to be their best location for plant facilities. Still, a network of tax havens have attracted many foreign manufacturers by offering them 10-year tax holidays.

• Even when local conditions favor certain manufacturers, a plant may be set up in the tax haven for many different reasons. The plant may manufacture and sell or lease its products to its parent company without tax liability. Or the tax haven company may manage the parent's foreign sales, helping the parent avoid taxes.

• The travel business is ideally suited for tax havens. Several retailers, for instance, may start their own wholesale travel business in a tax haven, such as Bermuda or the Bahamas, and funnel their Far Eastern business through their travel intermediary. The wholesaler's tax-free profits cannot be repatriated to America but can flow to most other countries.

• Speaking of the travel business, many tax-free havens give five or 20-year tax holidays for new hotels. Puerto Rico, Jamaica, Tunisia, Barbados, Haiti, Panama, the Dominican Republic, most of the British Caribbean islands and the French West Indies are only a few havens with this policy.

• Are you an inventor or writer? Royalties from patents or copyrights usually receive advantageous tax treatment if a tax haven company sublicenses other global companies. If the income accrues to the tax haven company, the income is not taxable. Ireland, for instance, does not tax the income of its artists.

- If your country taxes the current income of your foreign corporation, you can set up a joint 50/50 partnership with a tax haven company and accumulate income tax-free because the company is not controlled by either partner.

- A tax haven captive insurance company can re-insure or insure casualty risks and have unlimited premiums and interest income accumulate completely tax free. Its clients can be located worldwide.

- Banking and financial service profits in a tax haven are virtually tax-free because dividends, interest and capital gains are not considered taxable income to these firms. Similarly, trust funds and/or personal holding companies can be organized to hold foreign currencies or foreign currency assets. Nearly any kind of investment or asset can be sheltered in a tax haven to minimize or even completely avoid devastating estate taxes, which may foreseeably rise to 70 percent on estates over $200,000.

- A parent company can set up an export trade or commodity broker operation in a tax haven for worldwide sales or financing. Its discounts, commissions, advertising allowances and other direct or indirect profits will be completely tax free. By aggressively allocating the general and administrative costs, the parent company can realize even more significant tax deductions.

The list goes on.

Now you understand why global companies expand and diversify into the tax havens. Labor conditions and other economic factors seldom tell the

note Tax havens use tax savings as their carrot to attract industry.

entire story. Tax savings is an important part of that tale. Intelligently planned multinational companies grow faster when they have fewer taxes to pay.

These are, of course, only a few examples of how savvy companies save taxes by going offshore. While countless other examples apply to other industries, it should be clear that the opportunities are there. You need only find the one that's right for your company!

Tax implications of offshore trusts

The offshore or Asset Protection Trust and any entity it owns, such as the international business corporation (IBC), often utilized as a holding mechanism for investments, are non-U.S. persons and taxed as such. The United States taxes non-U.S. persons based on the concept of source jurisdiction and applies this concept to foreign corporations and non-resident aliens, such as foreign trusts.

In general, foreigners are subject to U.S. income tax only on the income sourced in the United States. Since the international business corporation is owned by the trust and the trust is not structured as a grantor trust, then the rules attributing ownership from foreign entities to beneficial owners thereof force you to consider the tax implications of the trust.

Normally you set up an Irrevocable Offshore Trust. Since the trust is a foreign trust, none of its undistributed foreign income will be subject to an income tax, either in the United States or the haven jurisdiction. There are two keys to qualifying as a foreign trust and thereby avoiding income tax. First, the trust must earn foreign source income. If the trust owns the Templeton Luxembourg-domiciled mutual funds, any income earned is considered foreign source income. However, if the trust owns the Templeton U.S. mutual funds, any income earned is considered U.S. source income and subject to a flat 30 percent withholding tax at the source. The Luxembourg funds are incorporated beyond America's shores, and income earned from the funds need not be reported to any government because of the structure of the trust and treasury regulation under which the trust operates. The trust is not obligated to report any earnings and the Templeton group does not issue information returns on its Luxembourg funds. Information returns are issued on American funds, however. Several Templeton Luxembourg funds allow investment in American securities. But because this group was incorporated in the Grand Duchy of Luxembourg, it is considered an offshore entity and its income from investment in American securities qualifies as foreign source income and, therefore, is non-reportable.

Second, the trust must retain the foreign income it earns. If the foreign income is distributed as a salary or a management fee, for example, the distribution is subject to U.S. taxes.

> **HOT spot** The ability to allow funds to repatriate without triggering a taxable distribution is of utmost importance.

You can accomplish this scenario by using a deferred private annuity arrangement between the trust and the U.S. grantor.

note

A private annuity operates under rules similar to those regulating commercial annuities. In basic form, a private annuity is a 50-paragraph instrument that will sit in your safe deposit box after it is drafted. It is purely a private contract between your trust and the annuity holder to provide income at a future point to the trust beneficiary and usually contains the following features:

- Surrender: The policy may be surrendered at any time without penalty. The surrender value is the actual value of the account.

- Privacy: This instrument is a private contract between the annuity holder and the trust.

- Tax exemption: Under U.S. Private Annuity rules, American citizens can purchase these contracts and lawfully avoid all reporting requirements until such time as the funds begin payout as profit. This in effect defers all taxes until the maturity or surrender date, a future point in time.

- Loanback provisions: The loanback provisions are structured within the annuity contract to allow loanbacks of capital as needed.

- Investment management: This provision allows the annuity holder to choose his own investment manager.

- Signature authority: The trustee of the trust has signature authority over the segregated annuity funds.

- Maturity: At the time of maturity, the policy owner may roll over the proceeds into a new annuity.

- Beneficiary: The policy owner may appoint any individual or a trust as the beneficiary of the policy.

- Maturity date: The maturity date can be set at ten years after the date of issue.

The large U.S. insurance industry relies on these rules for its commercial annuities. You take the same set of rules to operate a deferred private annuity. There are no taxes until the maturity date is reached.

 Every year, tens of thousands of Americans receive tax-free income from their offshore trusts. They comply fully with U.S. tax laws and there is nothing the IRS can do to stop it until Congress changes the tax code. Review with your tax advisor the tax-saving opportunities an offshore trust provides you.

Tax-free offshore employment

As a tax-poor American, you can substantially increase your standard of living by completely avoiding all U.S. income taxes. Sound interesting? Countless Americans are legally doing just that. You can, too. How? Exploit a major tax loophole that lets you earn tax-free income offshore.

This loophole is the foreign-earned-income exclusion, or so-called "$70,000 exclusion." It allows Americans who live and work outside the U.S. to exclude, from their gross taxable income, up to $70,000 of foreign-earned income, plus employer-furnished housing allowances. There are also other tax breaks. For example, each married spouse working overseas can exclude $70,000 in salary, so $140,000 in income, plus housing allowances, becomes tax-free income to a married American couple who lives and works outside the United States. Note that this is not a tax deduction, credit or deferral. It is an outright exclusion of this income from your taxable gross income!

To gain these big tax benefits you must fully satisfy three IRS rules:

1) You must have your "tax home" in a foreign country.

2) You must pass either a "foreign-residence test" or "physical-presence test."

3) You must have earned your income from within the haven.

If you work overseas but reside in the United States, your tax home is in the U.S. So to qualify for the foreign-earned-income exclusion, you must prove that you both work and live outside the United States.

An executive, for example, may work at a foreign plant while his family remains at their U.S. home. They do not qualify for the offshore employment loophole because the couple did not establish a foreign tax home. To qualify, you must sell or rent your U.S. home and establish your primary residence outside the United States. There is also the physical-presence test that provides that you must stay abroad for 330 days—whether or not consecutive—within a 12-month period. Other rules complicate this rule. For instance, an overseas assignment may overlap two tax years, requiring the $70,000 exclusion to be prorated over both tax years.

The foreign-residence test is easier for most Americans because they only need to show that they are truly residents of the foreign country for the required time, and with the intent to remain indefinitely. How does the IRS determine "intent"?

- **Permanency of residency:** Transients reside in hotels; residents own homes or have long-term leases.

- **Personal belongings:** The more personal possessions you take offshore, the stronger your case. Leaving personal items in the U.S. shows an intent to remain a U.S. resident.

- **U.S. property:** A vacant U.S. residence shows an intent not to permanently leave the United States for foreign residence. Selling or renting a U.S. residence shows an opposite intent.

- **Legal documents:** Obtaining a foreign driver's license, foreign voter registration, and foreign last will and testament will help. Maintaining your U.S. license and voter registration will hurt.

- **Local involvement:** Become at least as involved in community activities in the foreign country as you were in the United States.

- **Foreign taxes:** Foreign countries usually tax their residents. But if you claim an exemption from local taxes because of non-residency, you then inadvertently admit to U.S. residency. This explains why Americans often prefer to qualify under the physical-presence test rather than under the foreign-residence test. Under the physical-presence test you can disclaim residency of the foreign country and still claim exemption from that country's taxes—while simultaneously avoiding U.S. taxes.

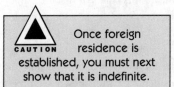

Once foreign residence is established, you must next show that it is indefinite.

Future plans to return to the United States disqualify you as a foreign resident. The IRS will consider your employment contract because short-term contracts show a future intent to return to America while open-ended or renewable contracts will more easily qualify you as a foreign resident. The IRS also examines other characteristics of your job or factors to reflect intent. This does not mean you cannot make frequent trips to the United States without jeopardizing your foreign-residence status. You can.

You must next identify income that can be excluded. Not all income qualifies for the exclusion, only foreign-earned income. Foreign-earned income is income paid for work performed within a foreign country. This includes salaries, commissions, professional fees and tips. Interest, rents, dividends and capital gains do not qualify under the $70,000 exclusion.

Self-employed overseas? Professionals can generally exclude all their income—up to $70,000—but when both personal services and capital produce your income, no more than 30 percent of the net profits can be excluded.

Other non-qualifying income includes employer-furnished meals, lodging on the business premises, annuity payments, income to U.S. government employees, non-qualified deferred compensation, disallowed moving expenses and income received two years or more after it is earned.

The $70,000 exclusion applies only to federal income taxes. The Social Security tax still applies to salaried employees, and the self-employment tax to the self-employed. A salaried worker with a U.S.-based employer still has Social Security taxes withheld.

The $70,000 offshore loophole can save you a small fortune in taxes. While there are a few additional technicalities, a good tax lawyer or accountant can further explain the foreign employment loophole to you. If you think you would enjoy an adventurous year offshore, and pay absolutely no U.S. taxes on your income, you now have your formula!

Expatriates and tax exiles

Many Americans can't pay their federal taxes and live in the style they want, so they leave the country, give up their U.S. citizenship and take up residence in a haven with less burdensome taxes.

You would think they must be out of their minds to forfeit U.S. citizenship simply to escape our taxes, but they do. They are the tax exiles or expatriates. And their number grows daily. It is not done only to avoid income taxes, although for many ex-Americans that is reason enough.

The desire to escape estate or inheritance taxes is a more compelling reason to become an exile. A multimillionaire can lose 55 percent of his estate to federal estate taxes. Another 10 percent may go for state inheritance taxes. An elderly American with a sizeable estate may see

> **note** You can live in the Caymans or Bahamas and pay no income tax. A high-earner can lose about 40 percent of his income to taxes here in the United States.

relinquishing citizenship a fair trade-off for the chance to leave his heirs his entire estate rather than one-third his wealth. In fact, most expatriates are people in this position. And if the United States hikes its estate taxes to 70 percent, as has been repeatedly threatened, we can expect a tidal wave of exiles moving to the Caribbean.

It also is becoming easier to find a haven that will welcome an ex-American exile. Nevis, for example, requires you to buy $150,000 worth of local real estate and pay $50,000 in fees. In return, you have the satisfaction of knowing Nevis has neither an income tax or estate tax. Similar arrangements can be had in most other havens.

Expatriation is a comparatively easy choice for wealthier Americans who hold dual citizenship and whose wealth is already concentrated abroad.

While other countries may welcome you, this does not mean that Uncle Sam will let you—or your money—go quite so easily.

If the IRS suspects you are renouncing your citizenship to avoid taxes, it will attempt to tax your holdings for another ten years—no matter where you live. The burden of proving the expatriation was not for tax purposes falls on you.

Americans have parked their money offshore for many reasons: potential litigants, creditors, ex-wives, political unrest, economic instability, and privacy. Now they are parking themselves offshore to completely avoid Uncle Sam's tax collectors!

The best tax havens

Most popular are the no income tax havens. The Bahamas, the Cayman Islands and Bermuda are the most popular in this group.

Next in importance are havens with no foreign-source income tax. Some notables are Guernsey, Isle of Man, Cyprus, Gibraltar, Jersey, Liberia and Malta. Panama and Hong Kong also do not tax residents with foreign-source income, but these havens are less popular.

Tax havens that offer special tax benefits for regional offices of foreign companies include Greece, Jordan and the Philippines. For instance, the Philippines waives all taxes for foreign firms that buy at least $50,000 annually from Philippine firms. There are also a host of special purpose tax havens. For example, Austria and Luxembourg both feature tax laws that favor the formation of holding companies and international investment funds. The Netherlands is ideal for finance companies, holding companies and companies with royalty income.

Each haven has its own tax characteristics. It is important to clearly understand the tax laws of each haven so you select the one that can best shelter your wealth.

Key points to remember

◆ Tax havens can help you reduce, defer or eliminate taxes through legal or illegal means. Stay honest. There are ample tax-saving opportunities offshore without breaking the law.

◆ Offshore tax planning is complex. You will need a qualified offshore tax specialist to guide you and keep you within the law.

◆ You can set up offshore corporations and trusts that can provide you with considerable tax savings.

◆ You can work offshore and pay absolutely no income taxes on a $70,000 a year income.

◆ If you give up your U.S. citizenship and move to a no-tax haven, you may save a fortune in income and estate taxes. Is it worth the price?

The secrets
of offshore
banking

7

Chapter 7

The secrets of offshore banking

All havens have a mixed collection of domestically and foreign-controlled institutions with varied customer bases and business purposes.

HOT spot Selecting the right offshore bank is as important as selecting the right offshore haven.

You should not believe that offshore banks are necessarily smaller banks. The world's largest and most progressive banking institutions can be found offshore. They often reach that status because they can best thrive in the offshore environment that both attracts depositor money and encourages progressive banking services to sophisticated customers who expect more services. The big banks include the giant Swiss banks—Credit Suisse, Swiss Bank Corporation, Union Bank of Switzerland. Leading American banks include Chase Manhattan, Citibank, Bank of America and, of course, the English banks: Barclays and Westminster.

The havens also are dotted with thousands of private banks that do not advertise for deposits, publish no financial statements nor are anything more than brass-plated names on doors.

Some havens, such as Switzerland, have banking regulations as rigid as those in the United States. Smaller, newer havens impose less regulation on their banks. This encourages the startup of private banks but can mean less safety for a depositor.

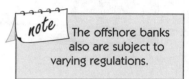
note The offshore banks also are subject to varying regulations.

How to choose an offshore bank

The starting requirement is to pick a financially strong bank. Some offshore banks are notoriously wobbly. So you must thoroughly investigate the bank's financial condition—even if it is one of the largest and oldest. You can easily review a bank's most recent financial statements by reading *Polk's Directory of International Banks*, available at your local library.

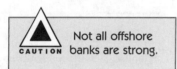
CAUTION Not all offshore banks are strong.

For Americans contemplating the opening of an offshore bank account, the task of measuring the bank's financial condition is challenging. Like American banks, the offshore banks publish annual reports. However, their accounting rules are sufficiently different from American accounting rules to make their reports nearly incomprehensible.

In truth, there is no one indicator to test a bank's financial strength. As a practical matter, you should consider three factors.

1) The bank's assets and capital. The size of the bank's assets reflects its financial power. The size of its capital is even more significant because it measures the difference between its assets and liabilities.

2) The age of the bank. While longevity does not insure future financial stability, a well-established bank at least indicates it is not a fly-by-night operation.

3) Evaluate the bank's management. Study the bank's reports. What are its management philosophies? How does it view economic conditions? What are the bank's policies in light of those conditions? What is the background of its management? Long-established banks always seem safer than new startups, and larger banks also imply financial stability. But age or size does not necessarily insure financial strength.

> Regardless of how closely you investigate, I have found that the only way to reduce risk is to use several banks.

Also select your bank for its services. Choose a bank with the minimum services you would expect from your mainland banks:

- cash cards and credit cards

- cash deposits

- no references required to open an account

- correspondent banks in principal countries and major cities

- fast, easy deposits, withdrawals and money transfers

- a member of SWIFT

- mail-holds for depositors

- instructions by phone, fax or mail

 Some banks make withdrawals a hassle, with notarized letters of instruction, endless forms and other red tape to delay returning your funds for weeks. Look for a bank that accepts fax instructions using a secret code word for authentication. This is a bank that will give you a speedy withdrawal.

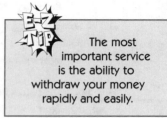

> **E-Z TIP**
> The most important service is the ability to withdraw your money rapidly and easily.

Another great banking convenience is the "all-in-one" account that provides:

- single and multiple currency checks—including Eurochecks

- global credit and debit cards, such as Plus and VISA

- easy transfer between savings and checking accounts

- interest rates tied to money market rates

- credit cards in alternative currencies

> **⚠ CAUTION**
> One bank you never want to do business with is one with branch offices or affiliates in the United States or its territories.

One bank may not offer every service, but do select a bank that features the services you want most.

The bank also should not keep its records (including computer processing) within the United States. Why? If the bank or bank records are located within the U.S., it destroys secrecy and privacy. Your records and bank accounts can then be seized by U.S. authorities or private litigants armed with court orders. Your offshore bank must have absolutely no ties to the United States, except for American correspondent banks.

Offshore banking charges vary widely, and this must also be considered when you choose an offshore bank. To attract depositors, many offshore banks—particularly Caribbean banks—draw depositors with "no charge" banking services. In the long run, these may be your most expensive banks.

Banking services cost the bank money, and one way or another the bank must recoup this expense. It may be a lower interest rate, stiff penalties for violating the bank's numerous and rigid rules, or temporary reductions, or waivers of charges, that are later hiked. Also banks with "no activity charge" or "no low balance charge" may be quite costly in other areas.

Offshore banking fees are generally competitive with onshore banks. The difference is that there is less uniformity with offshore fees.

CAUTION Shopping intelligently for an offshore bank is more important than shopping for a United States bank.

A treasury of offshore banking

Which country is best for offshore banking? Even investment specialists disagree on this question, largely because each haven offers different features. Do you mostly want privacy, security, or higher interest rates? Perhaps you most prize convenience, no local taxes, or safety. There are always tradeoffs.

Here's a brief rundown of the treasury of benefits that are available from banks worldwide:

- Hungarian, Cook Island, Nevis, Berlize, Caymans and Bahamian banks are favorites for absolute privacy. Bank accounts in these offshore havens are absolutely safe from prying eyes–including the IRS. Nearly half the American offshore accounts are sheltered in these popular havens. Their interest rates compare well with U.S. rates, but are below the interest rates paid in many other havens. Both are convenient and easily reached from east coast cities.

- Denmark and Austria rank high for interest and privacy. Moreover, their banks are financially strong and insure investment safety. Their privacy is good, but not quite as good as Switzerland, the Bahamas, Caymans or other British flag havens. Their two drawbacks are that

159

they are less convenient (but you can bank by mail) and deposits must be converted into their national currency.

• Scotland and the Isle of Man banks consistently pay the top interest rates. Security is also good. Privacy in the Isle of Man is not considered as secure as in other havens, but it is generally adequate. Near England, it is conveniently reached.

• The Philippines is the least safe country. It is also spotty on privacy, its banks are inconvenient to deal with and it is the least financially stable haven.

• Havens with tax-free banking include the Bahamas, Caymans, Turks and Caicos Islands, and Vanuatu. Low-tax countries are Bahrain, Bermuda, British Virgin Islands, Channel Islands, Hong Kong, Liberia, Liechtenstein, Monaco, Monserrat, Netherland Antilles and Panama.

• The tightest banking secrecy is in Antigua, Bahamas, Bahrain, Bermuda, Virgin Islands, Caymans, Channel Islands, Hong Kong, Isle of Man, Liechtenstein, Netherland Antilles, Panama, Singapore, Switzerland, Turks and Vanuatu.

• Mexico is the one most overlooked offshore banking center. Mexican accounts, unlike Swiss accounts, are not ordinarily "numbered" but nevertheless enjoy the same privacy. Mexican law makes it illegal for any bank to disclose banking information to third parties, and the Mexican government has no tax treaty with the United States or any other government. Mexican banking keeps your money beyond the range of the IRS and other creditors. Unfortunately, Mexican banks can be unsafe. Deal only with the *financiera*, or government-regulated banks.

HINT Figuratively and literally right beneath our noses, Mexican banks are as safe as Swiss banks and are equally secretive.

Other chapters detail the characteristics of the respective havens and Section Two profiles the more popular havens.

Myth and realities of Swiss bank accounts

Foreign bank accounts and Switzerland are traditionally synonymous. Swiss banking, like banking elsewhere, is perfectly legal for Americans. Neither the United States nor Switzerland restrict Americans' use of Swiss bank accounts. But does Swiss banking really beat banking in other havens? Here are some pros and cons to consider:

- **Convenience:** You can as easily transact business with a Swiss bank as an American bank. Swiss banks are very accessible, and their proximity to all European markets is a plus.

- **Financial stability:** Switzerland is easily the most stable tax haven. Switzerland has no exchange rules on precious metals or gold-backed currency, although they may someday prohibit these activities and restore foreign currency controls to help stabilize their economy. Swiss accounts can be excellent insurance against the collapse of the American dollar.

- **Privacy:** Swiss banks cannot legally disclose banking information to any government–including the United States. Disclosure of information under Swiss law is virtually impossible since accounts are numbered by code with the owner's name locked in the bank vault. Still, secrecy is not absolute. The Swiss can disclose banking information if they suspect criminal violations. Financial

> **HOT spot** Tax violations are not considered criminal under Swiss law so disclosure is never made by the Swiss to the IRS.

disclosures are also made in bankruptcy and inheritance cases. This is not so with other havens.

Swiss privacy is not as rigid as it once was, and many other havens afford more privacy. The United States has consistently pressured the Swiss to relax their secrecy, and they have done so on a number of recent cases.

The three safest Swiss banks are the Union Bank of Switzerland (Zurich), Swiss Credit Bank (Zurich) and the Swiss Bank Corporation (Basel). All Swiss banks are excellent but do not open an account in a bank with a branch or affiliate in America as this may destroy your privacy and asset protection.

Swiss banks offer savings and checking accounts, custodial accounts for your gold, precious metals, and stocks and bonds. Swiss accounts may be in either Swiss or American currency.

The Swiss numbered account has added to the folklore of Swiss banking. Much of the numbered account is myth.

All Swiss bank accounts are numbered, as are all bank accounts elsewhere. If requested, some Swiss banks will substitute an account name with a special code. The owner of the account is then known only to select personnel within the bank.

Thus, the only difference between a regular account and a numbered account is that ownership of the numbered account is known to fewer bank staff. From a legal and privacy standpoint, there is no difference between the two accounts. Any difference may be more psychological than factual.

The Swiss are not anxious to open new accounts to foreigners. Many Swiss banks insist upon a minimum account of $100,000. They also require identification and references. If you want a numbered account, you must meet personally with your banker.

Do not open a Swiss account only because of its reputation. Other havens outdo the Swiss, and they should be investigated.

Opening your offshore bank account

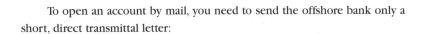

It's simple to open an offshore account, whether you handle it in person or by mail. To personally open your account, you need only travel to your offshore haven. The Swiss banks are not alone in requiring a personal interview. This is also true of many of the private banks in other havens. By visiting the bank to which you will entrust your money, you will build your confidence. The idea of entrusting your wealth to an unknown bank in a distant country might not seem too much of a risk.

To open an account by mail, you need to send the offshore bank only a short, direct transmittal letter:

> *Dear Sir or Madam:*
>
> *I enclose a money order for $xxxx (U.S. funds). I request that you establish a savings account under my below name and deposit this money order into said account. Please send any necessary forms and correspondence to me at the address below.*
>
>   *Sincerely,*_____

The bank will then send you the necessary forms to open the account along with literature describing the bank and its policies. You will also receive deposit and withdrawal slips.

As stated earlier, you cannot open a numbered account quite so easily in Switzerland. Swiss bankers scrutinize the backgrounds of numbered account holders to insure they are dealing with honest depositors, not criminals. So you must personally appear, and even then the Swiss do not always grant Americans a numbered account. Some Swiss banks now require Americans with numbered accounts to sign waivers that allow disclosure of their accounts to U.S. authorities. This, of course, destroys whatever value there is to Swiss banking.

You may be asked to sign several documents that are not required when opening an American account. One form is *The Declaration on Opening an Account*. Its purpose is to specify the beneficiary owner of the bank funds and the representative of the bank holder.

You should also sign a power of attorney that gives a third party the right to represent the account holder on all banking business. This is particularly useful if the account holder becomes incapacitated or dies. You will also be required to sign a signature card so the bank has your specimen signature.

If you are astute, you may observe that foreign banks generally do not ask for your Social Security number. This provides tacit assurance that the bank will not report your account or your earned interest to the IRS.

You can choose from many different types of offshore accounts:

- **Deposit accounts** compare to U.S. savings accounts, except that deposit accounts have restrictions on withdrawals that require you to post advance notice of any intended withdrawals above a determined amount.

- **Current accounts** are similar to U.S. checking accounts. Interestingly, many offshore banks do not issue checkbooks, however, this should not be of much concern to you because you would not normally pay routine bills from your offshore bank. Savings accounts pay higher interest than deposit accounts but have stricter requirements for withdrawing funds.

- **Investment savings accounts** pay even higher interest than savings accounts but are stricter on withdrawals.

- **Custodial accounts** are offshore safe deposit boxes.

- **Cash bonds** compare to U.S. certificates of deposit and commit your funds to the bank for a minimum period of time with penalties for early withdrawal.

- **Eurocurrency accounts** allow trade in other foreign currencies whenever the bank acts as your broker. Aside from differences between account features and names, there are several other notable differences between offshore and U.S. bank accounts.

Secrecy has never been a hallmark of American banks. Conversely, American banks emphasize lending. Offshore banks prefer to invest and attract capital. That's why the havens have so many different types of accounts. Offshore banks go that extra mile to please every potential depositor.

note — The difference is that offshore banks actually sell privacy and secrecy.

Operating your offshore account

Before you open your account, decide how much cash you will deposit offshore.

If you face no imminent financial or legal threat onshore, then start slow. Gradually shift your money overseas as your confidence and familiarity with offshore banking builds. But if you need fast judgment-proofing, you must quickly transfer all your cash to a safe haven.

Your federal income tax return also inquires about foreign bank accounts. Schedule B (Form 1040) in Part III asks:

> "At any time during the tax year, did you have an interest in or signature or other authority over a bank account, securities account, or other financial account in a foreign country?"

Disclosure of this information is mandatory. Civil and criminal penalties for not answering this question truthfully include a $500,000 fine or five years imprisonment.

Every U.S. citizen, resident, partnership, corporation, estate or trust that has signature authority or control over a foreign account must also report it to the U.S. Treasury (form TD F90-22.1) and file by June 30 of the year following any year in which there was such an account.

The annual report is waived where the aggregate account balances do not exceed $10,000 at any time during the year. All accounts must be included to determine whether the aggregate amount equals $10,000.

H
I)))   This information duplicates the foreign banking information on
N   Schedule B of the 1040 tax return, but its purpose is to have this information
T   available to all U.S. governmental agencies who may not easily obtain access to your tax return.

Accounts owned by offshore corporations and asset protection trusts may be exempt from reporting, even if they were established by an American taxpayer—if the taxpayer has neither signing authority or control over the account. This should be reviewed by tax counsel experienced with offshore accounts so that you neither inadvertently violate the law or unnecessarily report an account.

Despite the serious sanctions for violating the reporting requirements, more than half the tax returns are filed with the foreign account question unanswered. Because the IRS is overworked and burdened with more pressing compliance problems, they usually overlook it. The IRS is far less forgiving if you fail to report your offshore income.

Aside from these record-keeping requirements, there is no major difference between maintaining a foreign bank account and an American account, except for the goal to keep your offshore bank private and segregating transactions so prying eyes cannot discover your offshore account.

If your banking objective is total financial privacy, then you must observe these three key rules. So you do not create a trail that leads to your offshore account:

- Never directly transfer funds between your U.S. account and your offshore account. Transfer funds through an intermediary account–either an offshore company serving as a conduit or use untraceable cash deposits, traveler's checks, money orders or portable collectibles that you convert into cash deposits once overseas.

- Wherever possible, transact business with cash. Check this out with your offshore bank before you open your account because some offshore banks resist or refuse cash transactions.

- Use your offshore checking account and credit cards onshore only where you are not personally known. Your best bet is to never use them within the U.S.

How to use offshore plastic

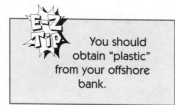

You should obtain "plastic" from your offshore bank.

This plastic may be a cash card, a debit card or a combination card, although they will probably be marketed under different names.

The cash card lets you withdraw cash from an automated teller machine, as you can with your mainland credit card. You can then withdraw funds with a minimum paper trail. It is also quite convenient. Because cash cards are international, you can gain access to cash in hundreds of countries. Major credit card systems include the PLUS cash card system (the biggest), the ETC cash card (most prominent in the Far East) and VISA (known everywhere).

The debit card replaces your offshore checking account and is very convenient. The debit card, like a credit card, debits your account. The difference, of course, is that with a debit card the bank does not extend you credit. This avoids the paper trail that invariably comes when you must establish credit.

All offshore banks issue credit cards, but in practice, many treat them as debit cards and require a compensating balance of two or three times your outstanding balance.

The more progressive offshore banks now issue combination cards, which serve as cash, credit and debit cards. They may also be used for check guarantees. This is recommended if you maintain $50,000 or more on deposit.

The one big danger with offshore plastic: it creates a paper trail, so never use your offshore plastic within the U.S. if privacy is your objective. Offshore plastic can also be troublesome if you are arrested and searched.

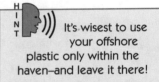

It's wisest to use your offshore plastic only within the haven–and leave it there!

Own your own offshore bank for big dividends

Tens of thousands of Americans own their own personal offshore bank. In most havens, the entire bank set-up can be handled for under $25,000.

For total privacy and asset protection, you can't beat owning your own offshore bank.

Would you like to be president of your own offshore bank? You can start your own bank from scratch, or buy an established bank. Starting a bank from scratch takes more time and effort. Buying an existing bank is less challenging but usually more costly. In either event, you will need good professional guidance to clear the red tape.

Where do you start? There are a number of firms that offer a low-cost program for U.S. investors who want to acquire or start their own offshore banks within a few days–and at a surprisingly low cost. You'll find them listed in the Appendix.

> **CAUTION** You are taxed in the United States for interest earned anywhere in the world. Failure to report foreign income is a crime.

Why should you own your own offshore bank? One reason is to guarantee your own privacy in case you have concerns about whether another bank can keep a secret. Most people believe an offshore or foreign bank offers tax protection, but this is not always true. What is true is that many offshore havens do not tax interest earned from their banks.

The basic tax avoidance strategy is to separate your money from yourself. To do this, you must transfer your offshore funds to a separate entity within the offshore haven, which entity is not subject to U.S. taxes, nor subject to taxes for its earned income.

Owning your own offshore bank is an excellent way to achieve this. Offshore banks are excellent tax insulators because they legally separate you from your money while allowing you to remain in control of your money in the offshore bank. Moreover, your offshore banking profits are not taxed by the United States until the profits are repatriated. Smart investors, of course, perpetually re-invest offshore to indefinitely defer their U.S. taxes.

> **note** Offshore bank ownership creates many more opportunities to avoid U.S. taxes than do any other offshore strategies.

While most havens impose no taxes on the income, profits or capital gains earned by their banks, haven bankers do pay a nominal annual license fee, ranging between $700 and $20,000. The average fee is about $5,000 with $10,000 an average initial fee.

Tax benefits for American-owned foreign banks

note

Did you know the IRS grants special privileges to American-controlled offshore banks? That's another big plus for owning your own bank.

For an offshore bank to be considered a bona fide financial institution, the IRS reviews the bank's activities with persons or companies that are not bank principals. But it's easy to qualify. Many American-owned offshore banks are no more than a name on a door, and only occasionally engage in an isolated transaction with unrelated third parties. American-owned offshore banks save their owners taxes in five ways—mostly through tax benefits granted offshore banks and not other American-owned corporations.

- **Exclusion from controlled foreign corporation tax penalties**

    If several Americans each own at least 10 percent of the bank (and together own more than 50 percent), that bank will be considered a Controlled Foreign Corporation (CFC), and its American shareholders must pay U.S. tax on their share of the bank's earnings, whether distributed or undistributed. However, the 1986 Tax Reform Act grants a special privilege to foreign banks owned by a single U.S. shareholder, which bank exports financing for its parent shareholder. Interest income from the financing exports on behalf of the bank's owner, is not subject to the CFC tax penalties. For the bank to avoid the CFC tax penalties-without limiting itself to export financing–U.S. citizens must own less than 50 percent of the bank.

One way to achieve this is for the bank to be at least 50 percent owned by a foreign partner. It will then not be a Controlled Foreign Corporation. You may also create a bank with 11 or more unrelated persons, each owning less than 10 percent. You can easily decontrol the bank using either method. You may, for instance, have 10 friends or business associates each own less than 10 percent of the bank, or sell ownership of the bank to 10 key customers. Or you may enlist depositors to be minority bank shareholders. Of course, you must be certain no American ever has more than 10 percent ownership in the bank.

- **Exemption from accumulated earnings tax**

  Offshore corporations are ordinarily subject to excess tax rates on undistributed U.S.-source earnings that are above $150,000 a year, because accumulated earnings over this amount are considered unnecessary to operate the corporation. Private offshore banks are usually exempt from this excess tax because offshore banks must accumulate their earnings for investment.

- **Deferral of foreign investment company tax**

  U.S. shareholders of any offshore corporation, including a bank, are taxed on their share of the corporation's passive income that exceeds 75 percent of its total income. This tax also applies to offshore banks, but payment of this tax on passive foreign investment company or bank income can be deferred until the income is repatriated.

- **Exemption from U.S. tax on foreign-source income**

  An ordinary foreign corporation must pay a U.S. tax on foreign-source income that is effectively connected with a U.S. business. However, private offshore banks are usually exempt from the foreign-source income tax because their activities are largely

171

handled internationally through a resident agent or host-country directors.

- **Exemption from assets-used or activities test for dividends and gains from securities transactions**

Ordinary foreign corporations may be taxed on certain U.S.-source dividends and securities gains under the assets used or activities test.

A private offshore bank that conducts business outside the United States is exempt from U.S. tax under the assets used or business activities test because as a financial institution it is expected to largely trade in securities.

> *note* The private offshore bank deserves investigation.

As a financial corporation, it is the best way to gain big tax benefits because the bank enjoys special corporate status. Just as corporations reap special tax privileges over individuals, offshore banks gain special tax benefits over American banks and corporations.

When an account holder dies

The mention of a secret offshore bank account prompts most people to ask, "What happens to my offshore account when I die or become incapacitated?"

Of course, when your heirs or executors know about your foreign account, you follow the same procedures that you would use in liquidating an American account. Offshore havens readily deliver the account proceeds to the rightful representative of the account holder when presented proof of executorship.

An offshore account that is kept secret from everyone may well be dormant and unclaimed upon the death of the account holder. Offshore banks usually will do nothing to find successors to the account and will only follow the existing wishes of the now-deceased account holder.

For this reason, account holders must plan for the transmittal of their account proceeds upon their death. There are three recommended situations:

1) Set up joint and several accounts. The funds would then automatically be transferred to the co-owner upon your death. Of course, the co-owner must be someone you completely trust and whom you intend to receive the funds upon your death.

2) Grant a power of attorney so that someone may access your account upon your death or disability. As stated earlier, banks will encourage this arrangement when you open your account.

3) Have your offshore bank account owned by a trust or corporation so that a trustee or director has direct control over the account and responsibility to distribute the funds upon your death in accordance with your wishes.

Funds in offshore accounts are considered part of your estate for estate tax purposes. However, most havens do not impose an estate or inheritance tax on these accounts.

Key points to remember

◆ There are offshore banks of every size and purpose. It is as important to choose the right bank as the right haven.

◆ Swiss banks are not always preferred. There are some disadvantages with Swiss banking that many Americans overlook.

◆ Never transmit funds directly between your onshore and offshore accounts. If privacy is an objective, always transmit funds through an intermediary account.

◆ Consider the range of services a bank offers—as well as its financial strength.

◆ Owning your own offshore bank can save you taxes and provide more privacy.

◆ You must report to the U.S. Treasury offshore accounts totalling $10,000 or more.

The eight keys to offshore success

Chapter 8

The eight keys to offshore success

What you'll find in this chapter:

- ➠ Analyzing your objectives
- ➠ Obtaining professional advice
- ➠ Visiting your chosen haven
- ➠ Gradual investing
- ➠ Developing an offshore strategy

Now that you've nearly completed *Offshore Investing Made E-Z*, the question is how can you put it all together with an action plan to help insure your success offshore.

Quite possibly you already have some experience with offshore havens and only wanted to pick up a few pointers to become even more successful. I hope you gained those tips. If your offshore experience was less fruitful than you had hoped, then read this chapter closely. You may have shaped your offshore strategy incorrectly. Perhaps you had wrong or unrealistic expectations. You may have selected the wrong haven or offshore investments. You may have put too much or too little of your money offshore. As with any financial plan for investing your money at home, your offshore plan must be just as sound.

If you are going offshore for the first time, then you must step even more carefully. New offshore investors must move cautiously and intelligently. Offshore banking is not without its pitfalls, risks and hazards. Fortunately, serious problems can usually be avoided—but only if you follow what I consider to be the eight rules for offshore success.

Why these eight rules? Because I have watched countless novice offshore investors attempt to navigate their way through the waters of offshore banking. With or without professional guidance, some have enjoyed enormous success. The failures made serious blunders that cost them their fortune and forever soured them on the offshore experience. These blunders invariably were the failure to follow the eight key rules for offshore success that I now give to you:

Success rule #1

Decide whether offshore investing is for you

Offshore havens seemingly portray a financial opportunity offshore that is perfect for everybody. But that is not true. Not everyone is an offshore candidate. Many people, for a variety of reasons, are simply uncomfortable with the thought that their money is in a strange, distant land—an uneasiness usually traced to the myths about offshore banking that I tried earlier to dispel.

Some of these people can and will overcome their fears. They will move slowly and super-cautiously at first and become more active offshore as they become more comfortable. Yet others will never overcome their uneasiness. Nothing can quite bring these people to the point where they can comfortably take the offshore plunge.

If you are very uncomfortable with having your money offshore, then don't force the issue. But, do decide whether it is a matter of learning more or an insecurity that you will never overcome.

Even when I recommend going offshore, fewer than 50 percent of my clients venture overseas with their money. Regardless of the financial benefits, I cannot coax the others. Nor do I try too hard. You must be open to the idea from the start.

On the other hand, there are those who are too anxious to go offshore. They may overestimate the potential rewards, underestimate its risks or costs, or foolishly see it as a panacea for all their financial problems at home. If the reluctant need prodding, the over-anxious require restraint. Ask yourself five important questions:

1) How do you now feel about offshore investing?

2) What can you do to become more comfortable as an offshore investor?

3) How can you begin your offshore program so you are less fearful?

4) Do your professional advisors recommend that you invest offshore?

5) Does your spouse or family encourage or discourage offshore investing? Why?

Success rule #2

Set clear and obtainable objectives

You must next ask yourself why you want to go offshore with your wealth.

Only when you know what you want to accomplish can you select the right haven and correctly implement a plan to achieve those goals. Remember the expression, "To get there you must first know where you want to go." This is particularly true with offshore banking.

> **HOT spot** Understanding your objectives is pivotal to offshore success because you must tailor your strategy to meet specific financial goals.

What is it that you want to achieve offshore:

- Tax protection?

- Asset protection?

- Privacy?

- Higher investment returns and profits?

- Diversification and safety?

You may have other reasons for banking offshore. But, whatever your goals, make certain you understand them. Do you have several objectives? Prioritize them. How important is each? What trade-offs between these objectives will you accept? For instance, if your objectives are tax savings and asset protection, which do you value more? How much are you willing to sacrifice some tax benefits in return for greater asset protection? How much more are you willing to invest in fees and costs to gain more asset protection? These are also the issues you will want to explore with your spouse and others with an interest in

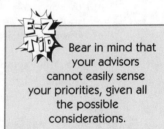

Bear in mind that your advisors cannot easily sense your priorities, given all the possible considerations.

your finances. You'll also want to explore with your professional advisors the trade-offs, as well as the possible alternatives that can more closely reconcile conflicting objectives.

Research your situation and you may discover that you can easily accomplish your objectives right here, at home, without sending your money offshore. Or, you may discover the cost and effort of offshore banking is not worth the marginal benefits it will give you in your situation.

Without solid objectives you are bound to fumble around in the international marketplace. You are almost certain to choose the wrong haven.

You may also select professional advisors who know too little about whatever you hope to achieve offshore.

You need specific strategies to achieve your objectives and specific tactics to achieve the strategies. It all comes back to knowing your objectives.

Don't set your objectives too quickly. Most Americans go offshore for one primary reason—tax avoidance, asset protection, privacy, higher investment profits or diversification—without considering other possible benefits.

> **E-Z TIP** While you may have your one big reason for going offshore, do keep an open mind to the other opportunities that await you.

The lawsuit-defendant, for example, who seeks asset protection may happily discover he can protect his assets, and with modest additional planning also save a bundle in taxes. Or, you may want to pursue investment opportunities overseas but only later realize you also can easily gain asset protection and privacy. Most offshore havens offer several possible benefits.

Success rule #3

Educate yourself

> *note* You must become that informed consumer!

Offshore investing takes know-how, and you can't leave it all to your professional advisors. You must personally know at least the basics of the game.

What you must do to educate yourself about the offshore world will, of course, depend on your offshore experience and planned involvement. While this book gives you the basic information you need to invest a few dollars in an offshore bank, you may need more. Do you plan to start an offshore bank? You will need considerably more expertise about the intricacies of offshore

181

banking and finance. You will at least need to read several good books about offshore banking. But, don't stop there. Talk to people who started their own banks in the haven under consideration.

On the other hand, if you expect to start an electronics plant in Mexico, you may spend months researching how to operate that business in that particular haven.

How do you become a serious student of offshore havens? Fortunately, there are many good books and journals to tell you everything you need to know about offshore havens. My library features over 30 excellent books on the subject from knowledgeable authors. I also subscribe to several offshore journals. My clients expect me to keep abreast of the newest developments in offshore banking, and offshore events change rapidly.

Build yourself a good reference library. Read all you collect. But don't accept everything you read at face value. In this game there is plenty of hype—particularly in journals that advertise selected havens or specific offshore services.

Talk to people! There are many more people involved with offshore havens than you may expect. Your professional advisors can probably put you in touch with a few. Or you may call my office for some names. I have many satisfied clients who will candidly talk to you about their offshore experiences. Of course, try to find people who closely share your objectives and have first-hand experience with the haven of interest to you.

Let me repeat: If you are to be a serious offshore investor, you must keep up with new developments. There are always new and more exciting opportunities, and, havens that once fulfilled your needs, may no longer be your best choice.

Offshore banks cannot legally advertise in the U.S., so you won't easily get good, current and usable information. That's why I suggest you subscribe to *Offshore Banking News*, the first and only news reporting service that researches offshore banking and financial opportunities, as well as changes in offshore laws and taxes. *Offshore Banking News* is also listed in the Resource section.

Success rule #4

Hire the right professional advisors

Even if you become sophisticated about offshore havens, it doesn't eliminate the need for good professional advice. Your offshore education only lets you work more effectively with your advisor. While the vast majority of people in my profession are honest, trustworthy and knowledgeable, every business has its crooks, incompetents and phonies. The offshore industry is no exception.

Good professional advice is absolutely essential, although selecting the right advisor can, in itself, be hazardous.

What should you look for in your advisor?

- **Professional status**

    Your best bet is to hire an attorney or CPA. While professional status hardly insures competence, it does at least give you some assurance the individual has sufficient honesty to keep his or her license. Licensure also implies the professional has some technical knowledge. Still, don't be mesmerized by credentials alone. Offshore investing involves many legal, financial and tax considerations that even the most conscientious practitioners will know little about, unless they also have had plenty of hands-on training.

- **Experience**

    Choose a consultant who is well-versed in the many different phases of offshore banking—from planning through implementation. You need a "hands-on" advisor, one who has walked the road before. It's a big plus if your advisor has accomplished your offshore objectives for others within the haven of interest to you.

    How many situations similar to yours has the professional handled? Can you get client references? (Do expect and respect confidentiality here.)

- **A wide resource network**

    Good offshore consultants rely upon a wide resource network. You especially want your advisor to be connected with key individuals, politicians and institutions within your specific haven. Good contacts are critical if you want to avoid problems and insure your plan is smoothly implemented. It helps enormously if your advisor knows the key government officials in your haven. This is particularly vital if, for example, you plan to open a bank or overseas business that is highly regulated or needs special permits. You may also need your primary advisor to refer you to other professionals, such as tax specialists or investment advisors. Larger, more complex offshore deals are usually a team effort.

- **Objectivity and the ability to meet your needs**

    Your offshore goals, circumstances and needs are unique. Nobody shares exactly your same situation. Your advisor must create the plan that's just right for you.

    You can't always find an advisor who will customize your plan. Many offshore consultants, for example, simply set up offshore companies or trusts in certain havens. Still, others only establish offshore banks, or handle only specific offshore investments. The offshore world is a niche business. I suggest that you start with a good generalist, one who can objectively design your offshore program.

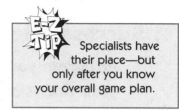

Specialists have their place—but only after you know your overall game plan.

It's a good idea to first meet your advisors with specific objectives or a game plan in mind. But, encourage other recommendations from your advisor. Then, probe their advice: Have they adequately explained the advantages and disadvantages? The costs? The time and travel required? The options and alternatives?

What will it cost to hire a good offshore advisor? Expect to pay about $150 to $250 an hour for an experienced consultant. Many will quote you a flat fee. By consultant shopping, you will better understand the available options and also obtain a surprising range of fees. Still, the lowest fee is not always your biggest bargain. A more expensive consultant may ultimately prove most economical, particularly if your advisor has the right connections and can help you avoid problems later.

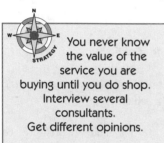

You never know the value of the service you are buying until you do shop. Interview several consultants. Get different opinions.

Where do you find a good consultant? The publications listed in the Resource section list prominent offshore consultants. In addition to my own Garrett Group, I have added several other excellent offshore firms. Check them out. These professionals are long-standing friends and colleagues who truly know the business of offshore banking, and I have found that they serve their clients exceptionally well.

Success rule #5

Integrate your offshore strategies with your financial planning

You probably won't have all your wealth offshore. You may have real estate and other onshore investments and assets. You must, therefore, integrate your offshore arrangements into your overall financial plans, and particularly your estate planning.

For these reasons, you must involve your financial advisors before you commit to an offshore strategy. Only then can you coordinate important financial issues that include:

- reducing your income and estate taxes

- passing your offshore assets on to your heirs

- control and repatriation of your offshore funds if you die or become disabled

> *note* Offshore banking is only one piece of your total financial future. That piece must fit perfectly with the other pieces.

Fortunately, offshore banking does not always signify adverse consequences. Offshore strategies frequently enhance your overall financial plans because they usually produce higher investment returns, lower taxes, or more satisfactory estate plans. In many cases, offshore banking is the catalyst for more effective financial planning.

Nevertheless, do anticipate both advantages and disadvantages as you redeploy your assets offshore. Once you understand the overall financial impact from offshore banking you can decide upon a game plan most in harmony with your various objectives.

Success rule #6

Personally check out your haven

My clients visit their chosen haven—before they send their money. I insist upon it. You can't really know a haven from books and magazines alone. You must go there and learn their customs and how they do business. You need to understand how their people think and get a sense of their politics, legal system, economy, and culture. You need to meet and talk to their bankers, business people, lawyers, accountants, and the many others you will do business with. You must see how easy or difficult it is to travel there, or even vacation there—if that is on your agenda. Only when you do these things can you invest in a haven with any confidence.

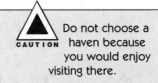
CAUTION Do not choose a haven because you would enjoy visiting there.

There is an upside to this advice. Offshore havens can be inviting vacation spots. Offshore investors frequently combine their offshore banking with fun tax-deductible vacations. But, do keep your priorities straight. First and foremost, your haven must meet your financial objectives.

How do you check out a haven once you arrive? Develop a relationship with a mentor who can help you network, someone who knows the ropes and can show you around. Pick someone from the haven with whom you are comfortable. As you become involved in the haven your mentor can be an invaluable resource.

Don't settle on a haven on the basis of one trip if you plan a substantial investment. Visit the haven several times. You can seldom learn everything you must know about a haven in a few days. Your perception of the haven may change over several visits.

The one danger of visiting an offshore haven is that your perception of a haven may camouflage its value as an offshore protector. Some of these havens

product does not constitute the rendering of legal advice or services. This product is intended for informational use only and is not a substitute for legal advice. State laws vary, so consult an attorney on all legal matters. This product was not prepared by a person licensed to practice law in this state. **187** are small, impoverished Caribbean islands. You would not think that such poverty-stricken countries are safe places for your money. From outside appearances they do not appear safe. But they are, for two reasons: 1) their financial institutions are remarkably strong, and 2) their laws are designed to protect you.

In large measure, all you are "buying into" is the haven's financial and legal system. The socioeconomics of the haven have little relevance to you. So when you do visit your haven, look beyond the poverty and squalor.

Success rule #7

Take the plunge

For every five people who think about investing offshore, only two actually do. Three fall by the wayside for a variety of reasons. Some procrastinate. Others fall victim to their fears. Still others become discouraged by the expense, time or effort required to make it happen. Then there are those who discover that the offshore havens won't accomplish their goals.

If offshore investing still makes sense to you after you thoroughly reviewed your situation with a good advisor, then by all means . . . proceed. Don't delay because you will only delay the financial benefits you hoped to achieve.

It's natural to be timid, even frightened, at first. I advise caution. Start small. Invest only a few dollars initially. Feel your way. Develop confidence. Learn the ropes gradually. When you are ready, invest more. But you must begin with that first important step!

Success rule #8

Continually develop your offshore strategy

Your offshore strategy should periodically change as your own circumstances and objectives change. Continuously adapt your offshore program to meet those new needs and capture those fresh opportunities that will assuredly present themselves if you keep your eyes open.

My clients frequently start with a modest offshore bank account. Gradually, they move all their money offshore. They diversify their investments into offshore securities or international mutual funds. They may have companies or trusts scattered throughout multiple havens. Some eventually establish their own offshore banks, investment houses, captive insurance companies or other more sophisticated offshore ventures.

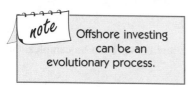

note Offshore investing can be an evolutionary process.

The point is that you must constantly reshape your offshore activities to fit your available resources, your growing confidence, skill and, of course, those new opportunities. In summary, you must maximize your offshore commitment to maximize your financial future.

These eight rules for offshore success don't tell the entire story. There's much more than can be said. In time you will learn the unwritten rules on your own, the way most people learn—by trial and error, and the expedient of experience. But, these eight rules are the essence of what it takes to get started in your own offshore program.

While all these tips are important to your success, none is more important than the need for good professional advice. Don't look for all the answers here. Instead, find that someone who can reinforce what you learned through this book with the specific advice you need for your situation.

CAUTION

Offshore investing can help you financially in so many different ways. The rewards can be truly enormous. But, so can the risks. As with everything, there are pros and cons to every offshore venture.

How well will you fare? There is only one way to find out: Try it! Offshore banking can open the door to a new and exciting world of financial opportunity.

Key points to remember

◆ Decide whether offshore investing is for you. You must be comfortable for it to work for you.

◆ Set clear objectives. Precisely what do you hope to accomplish with your offshore plan?

◆ Educate yourself. Learn what you can about offshore banking so you become an informed investor.

◆ Get good professional advice. Offshore banking can be complex and you will need an advisor to guide you.

◆ Coordinate your offshore arrangements with the rest of your financial planning.

◆ Check out your haven. It is the best way to gain confidence and learn about offshore banking.

◆ The only way to start is to take the plunge. Invest gradually but don't delay the process.

◆ Develop your offshore strategy. As with all financial planning, your offshore program must change with events.

Where to put your money and why

9

Chapter 9

Where to put your money and why

Each offshore haven has advantages and disadvantages. No two havens offer identical characteristics. One haven may provide superior tax advantages, while another has greater asset protection or secrecy. Some havens are more convenient for banking. Or, a haven may be more or less stable politically or economically. There are always trade-offs. You intelligently weigh the trade-offs and select the havens that can best suit your needs. But, you must consider all factors.

CAUTION

Many investors unwisely choose their haven on the basis of popularity or publicity. For instance, if you merely mention offshore havens, most folks immediately envision Switzerland, the Cayman Islands or the Bahamas. Their popularity, however, does not necessarily make them your best haven. In fact, these three havens differ markedly from each other in what they offer.

> **note** To choose your best haven, you must know what you hope to achieve and set priorities.

Once your offshore advisor understands your objectives, he or she may suggest several different havens. As a group, they can all satisfy your objectives.

 The most popular havens can be your worst choice. Havens that best suit your needs may be havens you've never heard mentioned.

For example, if you are after asset protection, your advisor may suggest you set up an Asset Protection Trust in the Cook Islands, the Turks and Caicos, Nevis, Gibraltar or Mauritius. These are all strong asset protection havens and the differences between them are minor.

If your goal is secrecy, your choice of havens would be Austria, Hungary or Liechtenstein.

Switzerland may be the most convenient haven for investing and the Channel Islands may best serve your tax goals.

This is why it is so very important to prioritize your offshore objectives. The matching process is critical to offshore success.

For example, you may set up an Asset Protection Trust in Nevis and have as its settlor a Bahamian company and as its beneficiary an international business corporation chartered in Mauritius. The trust may invest in

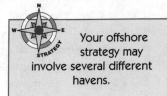 Your offshore strategy may involve several different havens.

Swiss Plus annuities—thus creating an offshore structure represented by four separate havens.

These multi-haven arrangements are quite common because they allow the planner to build a stronger offshore structure by use of different entities from different havens. While it may sound confusing, unwieldy and expensive—in practice, the multi-haven arrangement imposes little additional cost or complexity over the single-haven plan.

You must also stay abreast of the changes with the offshore havens. Their laws change as do their politics and economics. That's why havens rise and fall in popularity. The haven that may serve you best today may be a less desirable haven next year. You should periodically review this with your advisor so you can be relocated to a more favored haven should the need arise.

Ten key factors for choosing your haven

What factors should you consider when choosing your haven? It starts by matching your objectives to the haven that can best meet those objectives. Understand that each haven has its own unique character and specialization.

There are ten additional key factors to consider when selecting your haven. Some will be more important to you than others, but all must be evaluated if you are to choose the most advantageous haven. These ten factors are:

1) Tax structure

2) Tax treaties

3) Exchange controls

4) Stability

5) Legal system

6) Privacy

7) Asset protection

8) Investment opportunities

9)   Banking services

10) Convenience

Tax structure

It's no secret that considerable investor capital flows to offshore havens to escape confiscatory taxes at home. So, any haven worthy of the title must feature low or no taxes if it is to attract foreign funds. Every offshore haven described in this book has a favorable tax structure. Most have no tax on foreign deposits, which make them an ideal haven for foreigners to accumulate funds or conduct business, other considerations aside.

Tax havens tax their residents (individuals and corporations) at a higher rate than non-residents. This two-tier tax system gives the haven a stable tax base from its resident population and the ability to attract foreign capital through a low or no tax rate.

 Check the tax rate on foreign earnings for any haven that interests you. How do the taxes compare to those of other havens? How are corporations or companies taxed? Is it at a higher rate than individuals? *Also consider:*

How stable are the tax rates? What taxes are imposed—other than income tax? How costly are fees, permits and licenses? Are they so excessive that they are an indirect tax?

Tax treaties

Havens with tax treaties with the United States or other countries offer the advantage of no double-taxation, which means you do not pay taxes twice on the same income.

> *note*
>
> Tax treaties require you to pay one country or the other—but not both.

There is a big disadvantage with treaty havens: they usually have a Tax Information Exchange Agreement (TIEA) to encourage or require the interchange of tax information between the countries to facilitate tax enforcement and prosecution.

Havens that do not impose a domestic tax on outside investors have no need for a tax treaty, and they do not issue financial information to the United States or other countries. These are the havens you want for privacy.

Exchange controls

Exchange controls limit the flow of currency from one country to another.

Canada, Russia and Hong Kong are three countries that impose exchange controls. Their citizens frequently attempt to circumvent these restrictions because they often fear an economic or political downturn. "Flight funds," euphemistically called, always wind up in havens that allow the unrestricted movement of currency, whether in or out of the haven. As you would expect, few havens impose significant exchange controls.

Stability

A selected haven should be economically and politically stable. Investments may rapidly devalue without stability. Other investment and tax policies also may change so that the haven becomes undesirable.

note

Economic and political stability go hand in hand. You cannot have one without the other.

Havens can rapidly become unstable. Panama, historically a sound haven, lost stability through the political unrest of the Noriega regime. Mexico, another once-favored haven, is now less desirable because it has closer economic ties to the United States and greater information interchange.

Switzerland and other European countries, such as Liechtenstein and Luxembourg, have always demonstrated economic and political stability. The British crown colonies—the Bahamas, Caymans, Turks, Gibraltar and others— have reasonable stability because of their British affiliation.

Legal system

I prefer havens with a legal system based on the English common law. English common law has a long, predictable tradition. American law is based chiefly on English common law, and American advisors are comfortable with a legal system they are most familiar with.

Equally important are the haven's corporation laws. The simplified incorporation procedures, reasonable incorporation fees and protective corporate laws usually found in English common law jurisdictions are another big plus.

An advantage of an English common law haven is that it provides more confidentiality, privacy and protection for individual rights. These characteristics are not always found in other legal systems.

Privacy

Privacy is the essence of a good haven. The most highly prized havens have laws that guarantee their depositors financial privacy. These havens impose severe penalties on banking institutions that violate their rigid privacy requirements. Privacy can vary considerably between havens, so you must investigate this feature carefully.

Havens with treaties with the United States offer the least degree of privacy, Privacy must be absolute. Choose a haven that never shares information!

That is why Switzerland lost status as a favored haven—its treaties with the United States allow for the exchange of information in certain situations.

Asset protection

Protecting assets from domestic judgments, lawsuits, tax claims or divorce action is, of course, a popular reason for going offshore. But, havens vary markedly in how well they protect assets.

To start, check whether the haven recognizes asset protection trusts—as do the British crown colonies. Also check whether there are treaties with the United States that compel turnover of property to a bankruptcy trustee, the IRS or under criminal forfeiture proceedings.

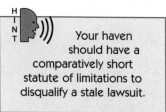

Your haven should have a comparatively short statute of limitations to disqualify a stale lawsuit.

You also want to check whether the haven recognizes the claim you seek protection against. Preferably, it will not. Finally, determine the statute of limitations for bringing a legal action within the haven.

Investment opportunities

In the vast international marketplace, all havens offer excellent investment opportunities. While all havens feature international banking, the better investment havens stimulate investment within their haven, particularly the less developed havens that want to develop industry and create more jobs.

> **E-Z TIP**
> To stimulate investment, havens offer an array of attractive investments and other concessions, such as tax holidays and grants.

Some of the emerging countries are quite aggressive in the concessions they grant to new industries. Mexico is one example, but there are others that have attractive deals for American firms looking to set up shop overseas.

Banking services

It may then be wise to establish your company within a particular haven, but, conduct your banking in another haven that has good banking accommodations. As stated, you should maintain a bank account in a jurisdiction other than where your company is chartered.

Don't expect the less-developed havens to compare to the world's money centers, but at the least they

> **HOT spot** Some otherwise excellent havens have notoriously poor banking services.

should offer several first-rate banks, access to the security exchanges, facilities for trading in the more sophisticated financial instruments—such as warrants and investment trusts—and a network of broker dealers.

Convenience

You must measure convenience in several different ways. Inexperienced investors consider location very important when selecting a haven. Yet, because so little offshore banking is conducted in person, the location factor is mostly psychological. People, understandably, want to be as close as possible to their money. This explains why Americans prefer Caribbean havens; the English, the Channel Island havens; and the Japanese, Hong Kong, Singapore or the Philippines.

Language is a more important factor. Americans are most comfortable with English-speaking havens. As a practical matter, most offshore bankers speak English, as do most attorneys and other professionals who serve foreign investors.

Transportation is a third factor. A nearby haven may be considerably more difficult to reach than a distant haven. But, as stated, travel to your haven can be an exciting side benefit of offshore banking when the haven is an alluring or leisurely vacation spot. This may disqualify Guam, the Cook Islands or Panama but the British Virgin Islands (BVI), Switzerland, or even the havens close to London can be fun places to visit your money!

Try to prioritize which of these factors are most important to you. Then research the various havens to determine which haven will best serve your needs.

You may have other factors to consider. Costs and filing fees may be a significant factor. For example, it may cost $400 to incorporate in one haven and $2,000 in another.

Key points to remember

◆ Each offshore haven has its own strengths and weaknesses. You must therefore choose a haven that will best satisfy your objectives.

◆ As the offshore havens change politically or economically or change their laws, they may become more or less desirable. That is why you must always stay abreast of changes in your haven.

◆ You must prioritize the features you most want from a haven.

Resources

••• Offshore Investing Books •••

Asset Protection Secrets

By Arnold S. Goldstein, Ph.D., published by Garrett Publishing, Inc., 384 S. Military Trail, Deerfield Beach, FL 33442

Building Wealth

By Adam Starchild, published by AMACOM Division, American Management Association
1601 Broadway, New York, NY 10019

The Caribbean Business Directory

Published annually by Caribbean Tunprint Directory Services
PO Box 350, Dept. D.C., West Falmouth, MA 02574

Everyman's Guide to Tax Havens

By Adam Starchild, published by Paladin Press
PO Box 1307, Boulder, CO 80306

Practical International Tax Planning

By Marshall J. Langer, published by Practicing Law Institute
810 Seventh Avenue, New York, NY 10019

Privacy, How to Protect What's Left of It

By Robert Ellis Smith, available thru amazon.com

Swiss Bank Accounts

By Michael Arthur Jones, available thru amazon.com

Tax Havens Encyclopedia

Published annually by Butterworth & Co. Ltd.
88 Kingsway, London WC2B, 6AB, United Kingdom
Distributed by Butterworth Legal Publishers:
St. Paul, MN; Seattle, WA; Boston, MA; and Austin, TX

Tax Havens of the World

By Thomas P. Azzara, published by Tax Haven Reporter
PO Box SS-6781, Nassau, Bahamas

••• Newsletters & reports •••

The Bahamas Financial Digest

Published by The Bahamas Financial Digest
PO Box N-4271, Nassau, Bahamas

Caribbean Business

Published by Caribbean Business
1700 Fernandez Juncos Avenue, stop 25, San Juan, PR 00909

The Economist

Published by, The Economist Newspaper Ltd.
111 W. 57th Street, New York, NY 10019

Financial Times

Published by Financial Times Publications
14 E. 60th Street, New York, NY 10022

Mark Skousen's Forecasts & Strategies

Published by Phillips Publishing Inc.
7811 Montrose Road, Patomac MD 20854

Offshore Financial Review

Published by
Offshore Financial Review
Greystoke Place and Fetter Lane
London EC4A lND, United Kingdom

Privacy Journal

Published by Robert Ellis Smith

PO Box 28577, Providence, R.I. 02908

Tax Haven Reporter

Published by Tax Haven Reporter

PO Box SS-6781, Nassau, Bahamas

••• Offshore Information •••

Business International

The Economist Intelligence Unit

Business International Corp.

90 New Montgomery Street,

Suite 1020

San Francisco, CA 94105

Croner Publications, Inc.

International Publishers

London Road, Kingston Upon Thames

Surrey KT2 6SR, United Kingdom

Scope Books, Ltd.

230 Peppard Road, Emmer Green, United Kingdom

www.scopebooks.com

••• On-line Resources •••

American Academy of Estate Planning Attorneys

http://www.aaepa.com

American Express Small Business Exchange

http://www.americanexpress.com/smallbusiness

BizProWeb

http://www.bizproweb.com

Center for Debt Management

http://www.center4debtmanagement.com

Certified Financial Planner Board of Standards (CFP Board)

http://www.cfp-board.org/index.html

Consumer Counseling Centers of America, Inc.

http://www.consumercounseling.org/about.html

Debt Counselors of America

http://www.dca.org/home.htm

Entrepreneur's Help Page

http://www.tannedfeet.com

Estate Planning Links

http://users.aol.com/dmk58/epl.html

Federal Trade Commission-Consumer Protection

http://www.ftc.gov/bcp/menu-credit.htm

Financial Management Association

http://www.fma.org

Financial Planning Interactive

http://www.financial-planning.com

Institute of Certified Financial Planners

http://www.icfp.org

International Association of Financial Planners (IAFP)

http://www.iafp.org

Garrett Publishing, Inc.

www.agoldstein.com/homcie4.html

Lycos Investments Guide

http://www.lycos.com/wguide/wire/wire_385880796_47240_3_1.html

MSN Money Central

http://moneycentral.msn.com/home.asp

National Association of Financial and Estate Planning

http://www.nafep.com

National Federation of Independent Business

http://www.nfibonline.com

National Foundation for Consumer Credit (NFCC), The

http://www.nfcc.org

Pension and Welfare Benefits Administration

http://www.dol.gov/dol/pwba

Small Business Administration

http://www.sbaonline.sba.gov

Small Business Advisor

http://www.isquare.com

U.S. Business Advisor

http://www.business.gov

U.S. Small Business Administration

http://www.sbaonline.sba.gov/starting

Yahoo! Business and Economy Companies Financial Services Asset Protection

http://dir.yahoo.com/Business_and_Economy/Companies/Financial_S ervices/Asset_Protection

••• Related links •••

Academy of Financial Services

http://www.umsl.edu/~eyssell/afs/afspage.html

American Bankruptcy Institute, The

http://www.abiworld.org

Association for Financial Counseling and Planning Education

http://www.afcpe.org

American Management Association

http://www.tregistry.com/ama.htm

Education Index, Business Resources

http://www.educationindex.com/bus

Inc. Online

http://www.inc.com

Internet Law Library

http://law.house.gov/329.htm

Links to Bankruptcy Related Sites

http://www.iimagers.com/bankruptcy.html

National Center for Employee Ownership

http://www.nceo.org/index.html

National Small Business Development Center (SBDC) Research Network

http://www.smallbiz.suny.edu

••• State Bar Associations •••

ALABAMA

Alabama State Bar
415 Dexter Avenue
Montgomery, AL 36104
mailing address:
PO Box 671
Montgomery, AL 36101
(334) 269-1515
http://www.alabar.org

ALASKA

Alaska Bar Association
510 L Street No. 602
Anchorage, AK 99501
mailing address:
PO Box 100279
Anchorage, AK 99510

ARIZONA

State Bar of Arizona
111 West Monroe
Phoenix, AZ 85003-1742
(602) 252-4804

ARKANSAS

Arkansas Bar Association
400 West Markham
Little Rock, AR 72201
(501) 375-4605

CALIFORNIA

State Bar of California
555 Franklin Street
San Francisco, CA 94102
(415) 561-8200
http://www.calbar.org

Alameda County Bar
Association
http://www.acbanet.org

COLORADO

Colorado Bar Association
No. 950, 1900 Grant Street
Denver, CO 80203
(303) 860-1115
http://www.cobar.org

CONNECTICUT

Connecticut Bar Association
101 Corporate Place
Rocky Hill, CT 06067-1894
(203) 721-0025

DELAWARE

Delaware State Bar Association
1225 King Street, 10th floor
Wilmington, DE 19801
(302) 658-5279
(302) 658-5278 (lawyer referral service)

DISTRICT OF COLUMBIA

District of Columbia Bar
1250 H Street, NW, 6th Floor
Washington, DC 20005
(202) 737-4700

Bar Association of the District of Columbia
1819 H Street, NW, 12th floor
Washington, DC 20006-3690
(202) 223-6600

FLORIDA

The Florida Bar
The Florida Bar Center
650 Apalachee Parkway
Tallahassee, FL 32399-2300
(850) 561-5600

GEORGIA

State Bar of Georgia
800 The Hurt Building
50 Hurt Plaza
Atlanta, GA 30303
(404) 527-8700
http://www.gabar.org

HAWAII

Hawaii State Bar Association
1136 Union Mall
Penthouse 1
Honolulu, HI 96813
(808) 537-1868
http://www.hsba.org

IDAHO

Idaho State Bar
PO Box 895
Boise, ID 83701
(208) 334-4500

ILLINOIS

Illinois State Bar Association
424 South Second Street
Springfield, IL 62701
(217) 525-1760

INDIANA

Indiana State Bar Association
230 East Ohio Street
Indianapolis, IN 46204
(317) 639-5465
http://www.iquest.net/isba

IOWA

Iowa State Bar Association
521 East Locust
Des Moines, IA 50309
(515) 243-3179
http://www.iowabar.org

KANSAS

Kansas Bar Association
1200 Harrison Street
Topeka, KS 66601
(913) 234-5696
http://www.ink.org/public/cybar

KENTUCKY

Kentucky Bar Association
514 West Main Street
Frankfort, KY 40601-1883
(502) 564-3795
http://www.kybar.org

LOUISIANA

Louisiana State Bar Association
601 St. Charles Avenue
New Orleans, LA 70130
(504) 566-1600

MAINE

Maine State Bar Association
124 State Street
PO Box 788
Augusta, ME 04330
(207) 622-7523
http://www.mainebar.org

MARYLAND

Maryland State Bar Association
520 West Fayette Street
Baltimore, MD 21201
(301) 685-7878
http://www.msba.org/msba

MASSACHUSETTS

Massachusetts Bar Association
20 West Street
Boston, MA 02111
(617) 542-3602
(617) 542-9103 (lawyer referral service)

MICHIGAN

State Bar of Michigan
306 Townsend Street
Lansing, MI 48933-2083
(517) 372-9030
http://www.michbar.org

MINNESOTA

Minnesota State Bar Association
514 Nicollet Mall
Minneapolis, MN 55402
(612) 333-1183

MISSISSIPPI

The Mississippi Bar
643 No. State Street
Jackson, Mississippi 39202
(601) 948-4471

MISSOURI

The Missouri Bar
P.O. Box 119, 326 Monroe
Jefferson City, Missouri 65102
(314) 635-4128
http://www.mobar.org

MONTANA

State Bar of Montana
46 North Main
PO Box 577
Helena, MT 59624
(406) 442-7660

NEBRASKA

Nebraska State Bar Association
635 South 14th Street, 2nd floor
Lincoln, NE 68508
(402) 475-7091
http://www.nebar.com

NEVADA

State Bar of Nevada
201 Las Vegas Blvd.
Las Vegas, NV 89101
(702) 382-2200
http://www.nvbar.org

NEW HAMPSHIRE

New Hampshire Bar
Association
112 Pleasant Street
Concord, NH 03301
(603) 224-6942

NEW JERSEY

New Jersey State Bar
Association
One Constitution Square
New Brunswick, NJ 08901-1500
(908) 249-5000

NEW MEXICO

State Bar of New Mexico
121 Tijeras Street N.E.
Albuquerque, NM 87102
mailing address:
PO Box 25883
Albuquerque, NM 87125
(505) 843-6132

NEW YORK

New York State Bar Association
One Elk Street
Albany, NY 12207
(518) 463-3200
http://www.nysba.org

NORTH CAROLINA

North Carolina State Bar
208 Fayetteville Street Mall
Raleigh, NC 27601
mailing address:
PO Box 25908
Raleigh, NC 27611
(919) 828-4620

North Carolina Bar Association
1312 Annapolis Drive
Raleigh, NC 27608
mailing address:
PO Box 12806
Raleigh, NC 27605
(919) 828-0561
http://www.barlinc.org

NORTH DAKOTA

State Bar Association of North
Dakota
515 1/2 East Broadway, suite 101
Bismarck, ND 58501
mailing address:
PO Box 2136
Bismarck, ND 58502
(701) 255-1404

OHIO

Ohio State Bar Association
1700 Lake Shore Drive
Columbus, OH 43204
mailing address:
PO Box 16562
Columbus, OH 43216-6562
(614) 487-2050

OKLAHOMA

Oklahoma Bar Association
1901 North Lincoln
Oklahoma City, OK 73105
(405) 524-2365

OREGON

Oregon State Bar
5200 S.W. Meadows Road
PO Box 1689
Lake Oswego, OR 97035-0889
(503) 620-0222

PENNSYLVANIA

Pennsylvania Bar Association
100 South Street
PO Box 186
Harrisburg, PA 17108
(717) 238-6715

Pennsylvania Bar Institute
http://www.pbi.org

PUERTO RICO

Puerto Rico Bar Association
PO Box 1900
San Juan, Puerto Rico 00903
(787) 721-3358

RHODE ISLAND

Rhode Island Bar Association
115 Cedar Street
Providence, RI 02903
(401) 421-5740

SOUTH CAROLINA

South Carolina Bar
950 Taylor Street
PO Box 608
Columbia, SC 29202
(803) 799-6653
http://www.scbar.org

SOUTH DAKOTA

State Bar of South Dakota
222 East Capitol
Pierre, SD 57501
(605) 224-7554

TENNESSEE

Tennessee Bar Assn
3622 West End Avenue
Nashville, TN 37205
(615) 383-7421
http://www.tba.org

TEXAS

State Bar of Texas
1414 Colorado
PO Box 12487
Austin, TX 78711
(512) 463-1463

UTAH

Utah State Bar
645 South 200 East, Suite 310
Salt Lake City, UT 84111
(801) 531-9077

VERMONT

Vermont Bar Association
PO Box 100
Montpelier, VT 05601
(802) 223-2020

VIRGINIA

Virginia State Bar
707 East Main Street, suite 1500
Richmond, VA 23219-0501
(804) 775-0500

Virginia Bar Association
701 East Franklin St., Suite 1120
Richmond, VA 23219
(804) 644-0041

VIRGIN ISLANDS

Virgin Islands Bar Association
P.O. Box 4108
Christiansted, Virgin Islands
00822
(340) 778-7497

WASHINGTON

Washington State Bar
Association
500 Westin Street
2001 Sixth Avenue
Seattle, WA 98121-2599
(206) 727-8200

http://www.wsba.org

WEST VIRGINIA

West Virginia State Bar
2006 Kanawha Blvd. East
Charleston, WV 25311
(304) 558-2456

http://www.wvbar.org

West Virginia Bar Association
904 Security Building
100 Capitol Street
Charleston, WV 25301
(304) 342-1474

WISCONSIN

State Bar of Wisconsin
402 West Wilson Street
Madison, WI 53703
(608) 257-3838

*http://www.wisbar.org/
home.htm*

WYOMING

Wyoming State Bar
500 Randall Avenue
Cheyenne, WY 82001
PO Box 109
Cheyenne, WY 82003
(307) 632-9061

Appendix

AUSTRIA

AT A GLANCE...

Capital
Vienna

Commercial Center
Vienna

Location
Austria borders Germany and Czechoslovakia to the north, Italy and Yugoslavia to the south, Hungary to the east and Switzerland to the west.

Climate
The climate is similar to the northeastern United States.

Population
The population is 7.6 million.

Language
The official and spoken language is German.

Currency
The unit of currency is the schilling.

Communications
Communications are excellent.

OVERVIEW

As one of the wealthiest industrial nations in the world, Austria is known as the gateway to eastern Europe. Investment activity is high: 22.4 percent of the gross domestic product. Austria is the axis of international business in Eastern Europe and a favorite for investors attracted to its high level of investment secrecy.

Austria is a neutral country with strong trade ties to Eastern Europe. It is not a member of the European Community (EC) and therefore is not subject to common tax policy.

LEGAL SYSTEM

The legal system provides for separate judicial and administrative functions and is based on the Federal Constitutional Act of 1920.

GOVERNMENT

Austria is a parliamentary democracy consisting of nine provinces. The three branches of the government are the executive, the legislative and the judicial. The executive branch includes the federal president, the chancellor and the cabinet. The legislative branch is represented by a bicameral federal assembly.

Judicial bodies include the constitutional court, the administrative court and the supreme court. Executive and legislative powers are divided between the federal government and the provinces.

INVESTMENT PROFILE

The main banking establishment of Austria is the Austrian National Bank. It has the power to influence Austrian economy and markets. Austrian banks, regulated by Section 23 of the Austrian Banking Act, preserve a high level of secrecy. Password accounts rather than numbered accounts are used. Only in certain extreme circumstances may Austrian banks disclose information about their clients.

Austrian banks can arrange a variety of investments including stocks, mutual funds, CDs, participation and profit-sharing certificates, bearer bonds, bearer mortgages and local-authority bonds.

Austria is not a good offshore center for incorporating. Foreign companies should operate under the limited-liability company or the stock corporation.

TAXATION

Austria has an extensive system of double taxation agreements with nearly 40 countries. In 1989, corporate taxation was reduced to 30 percent.

If a corporation has a holding in an affiliated company, all of the parent company's profit sharing is tax exempt.

Another tax break: the international inter-company tax concession. An Austrian corporation is exempt from paying Austrian corporation tax on any form of profit-sharing from a holding in a foreign corporation provided the following conditions are met:

1) The foreign corporation must be a corporation (not a partnership or other form of enterprise).

2) the Austrian corporation can show direct possession of at least 25 percent of a holding interest.

An Austrian holding company may then collect tax-free dividends from its foreign subsidiaries. The tax concession covers both disclosed dividend payouts and disguised profit distribution. Tax exemption for capital gains applies only to holdings in foreign companies—capital gains generated from Austrian corporations are subject to taxation.

BAHAMAS

AT A GLANCE...

Capital
Nassau

Commercial Center
New Providence, Nassau

Location
The Bahamas is made up of 700 islands and 2,000 cays scattered over 100,000 square miles and is located 50 miles off the Florida coast. New Providence Island, site of the capital city of Nassau, has an area of 83 square miles. The second largest city, Freeport, is on Grand Bahamas island.

Climate

The climate is moderate and ranges from 70° to 80°F.

Population

The population is 250,000. The majority of the population lives on the island of New Providence and Grand Bahamas. Many of the islands are uninhabited due to the lack of fresh water.

Language

The official and spoken language is English.

Currency

The unit of currency is the Bahamian dollar.

Communications

The Bahamas has excellent communications. Thirteen airlines fly to the Bahamas and direct flights are available from most international cities. Miami is 30 minutes away by plane and New York is approximately a three-hour journey.

Seventeen shipping lines connect the Bahamas with important world markets. Nassau has a major deep-water port and Freeport, on Grand Bahamas Island, has a fine natural harbor.

Freeport's owners hope that the port, which is as close to Miami as it is to Nassau, can be developed into a major regional hub for container shipments to North and South America, the Caribbean and Europe. The Bahamas has an excellent overseas telephone service which includes direct dialing to the United States and Canada.

OVERVIEW

Economically, the Bahamas thrive on tourism and the tax-haven industry. It is a popular vacation spot and gambling, shopping and fishing are enjoyed by tourists and residents alike.

Offshore haven activities dominate the financial world of the Bahamas. Financial services include international business companies, insurance companies, banks, personal investment companies, ship registration and trust services.

LEGAL SYSTEM

Bahamian law is based on British common law but is augmented by Bahamian statutes. The supreme court is the highest tribunal, the court of appeals occupies the middle position and the magistrates court has jurisdiction in minor civil disputes and criminal offenses. The ultimate court of appeals is the privy council of the United Kingdom.

GOVERNMENT

The Bahamas were initially settled in 1640 by the Eleutherian Adventurers, a group of Englishmen who sailed from Bermuda. The Bahamas has had a representative form of government since the 17th century.

In July 1973, the Bahamas achieved its goal of becoming an independent country within the British Commonwealth. A Governor-General appointed by the British government is responsible for defense, external affairs and internal security. However, the real head of the government is an elected prime minister who consults with a cabinet of nine ministers chosen from the legislature. The bicameral legislature has a 49-member house of assembly and a 16-member senate.

INVESTMENT PROFILE

Lawyers, accountants, stockbrokers, bankers and financiers are highly qualified and available in abundance. Bahamian banks have freedom from statutory reserves and liquidity requirements, permitting great flexibility. A host of excellent banking and trust facilities are available.

One benefit of setting up a tax haven in the Bahamas are Bahamian International Business Companies (IBCs). IBC advantages include:
- 24-hour formation subject to name approval
- Limited liability
- No minimum capital requirements
- Total tax-exemption for 20 years
- Minimal compliance work
- Director and shareholder anonymity

Companies limited by shares and companies limited by guarantee are the two basic types of corporations operating in the Bahamas. Companies limited by shares have fixed, unmodifiable authorized capital. They cannot buy back their own stock.

Companies limited by guarantee can reduce their share capital by buying back their shares and canceling them. Therefore, offshore funds are incorporated in the Bahamas as companies limited by guarantee.

TAXATION

The Bahamas do not have any tax treaties to avoid double taxation because it does not have any form of direct taxation. The main source of government revenue comes from customs duties and import taxes.

The Bahamas have no personal, corporate, profit, capital gains, estate, death or withholding tax.

BARBADOS

AT A GLANCE...

Capital
Bridgetown

Commercial Center
Bridgetown

Location
Barbados is an eastern island in the Lesser Antilles and is approximately the size of Texas. Haiti, Jamaica and the South American coast are all nearby.

Climate
The climate ranges from 80° to 85°F.

Population
The population of Barbados is approximately 300,000.

Language
The official and spoken language is English.

Currency
The unit of currency is the Barbadian dollar.

Communications
Barbados has excellent communications including world-wide direct dialing, facsimile and telex capabilities as well as overnight courier services.

OVERVIEW

Political and social stability has given Barbados a competitive edge over other tax havens. Harmonious transitions between the two opposing parties has contributed to its all-important reputation for being stable and has helped create an ideal base to expand free enterprise. Today, the economy is diversified into four primary industries: agriculture, tourism, offshore financial services and manufacturing.

LEGAL SYSTEM

The mature legal system is the product of English common law enacted by local parliament and upheld by local courts. The privy council in England is the highest judicial body, responsible for handling final appeals from Barbadian courts.

GOVERNMENT

Barbados became known as "Little England" as a result of its stature as one of Britain's first overseas possessions. The island also is home to the second oldest parliament outside of England.

The island was settled in 1627 but it wasn't until 1885 that it became a Crown colony. England reigned over Barbados until November of 1966 when it gained independence as a self-governing state within the British Commonwealth.

The essential powers granted the governor in 1652 became the basis for the constitution that went into effect in 1966. It remains the foundation for today's Westminster parliamentary system.

The governor general is appointed by the British monarch, both of whom are members of the Barbadian parliament. The senate has 21 appointed members and the house of assembly has 27 elected members.

INVESTMENT PROFILE

Barbados offers numerous tax incentives to attract investment capital. These programs have directly contributed to the growth of the economy. Tax concessions are the primary form of investment incentive available to all foreign investors.

The government is encouraging foreign investment in Barbados, with particular emphasis on manufacturing, tourism and low-tax offshore business.

The Central Bank of Barbados was organized in 1972 to stabilize the economy. The banks maintain proper levels of foreign exchange reserves, control the money supply, provide rediscount facilities for lending to industry and oversee bank activities, including establishment of reserve minimums.

There are two distinct types of entities in Barbados: the company and the public company. A company (formerly a private company) is considered a "small enterprise" if its gross reserves or assets do not exceed U.S. $500,000. Liability is limited by shares and the company has the right to restrict shares. Information disclosure is minimal. A single shareholder, director and incorporator are permitted. Most tax havens do not make the public company distinction. And then again, most do not have their own stock exchange for trading shares.

Anonymity can be achieved by purchasing an "off-the-shelf" corporation or engaging local professionals to form the company. The management firm will appoint local directors. Names of actual principals need not be disclosed.

TAXATION

Barbados does have taxes that produce revenue. However, the offshore financial sector pays almost no taxes. Most insurance companies and foreign sales corporations pay no taxes on their income. International business companies and offshore banks are taxed at a maximum rate of 2.5 percent on net income. Shipping corporations don't pay taxes for 10 years. The United States presently has double-taxation treaties with Barbados. The U.S. treaty with Barbados is one of the few tax-reducing treaties that the United States has with a low-tax jurisdiction.

BELIZE

AT A GLANCE...

Capital
Belmopan

Commercial Center
Belize City

Location
Belize is located on the Caribbean seaboard of Central America. It has an area of approximately 9,000

square miles, and is bounded by Mexico to the north and Guatemala to the west and south.

Climate
The climate is subtropical with an average temperature of 80°F.

Population
The population of Belize is approximately 200,000 with 60,000 living in Belize City.

Language
The official and spoken language of Belize is English although Spanish is widely spoken.

Currency
The unit of currency is the Belize dollar with a fixed exchange rate of BZ $1 to U.S. $1.

Communications
The Philip S.W. Gordon International Airport near Belize City has a recently constructed terminal building providing daily services through four international carriers to the United States and Central America. Telephone, facsimile and telex communications to and from Belize are excellent with international direct dialing facilities.

A satellite earth station at the capital Belmopan provides high quality telecommunication services throughout the world. International courier services for express delivery are well established.

OVERVIEW

Tourism has become a development priority and the government has favorable IBC legislation that attracts much offshore financial activity.

LEGAL SYSTEM

The law of Belize is derived from English common law supplemented by local legislation. The court system also is similar to that in England, and contract and commercial law is based on an English law model.

GOVERNMENT

Belize has a long history of peace, stability and democracy. It became a British Crown colony in 1862 and achieved complete self-rule in 1981. Belize is a member of the British Commonwealth, the United Nations and the Non-Aligned Movement.

The political system is based on the head of state British Westminster model with H.M. Queen Elizabeth II being represented by a Belizean governor general. Executive authority is exercised by the cabinet under the leadership of the prime minister, subject to approval by a 28-member house of representatives. In addition, there is an eight-member senate with the majority appointed on the recommendation of the prime minister.

There are two main political parties. In the last election, the government changed to the People's United Democratic Party after five years of rule by the United Democratic Party.

Both parties are committed to the economic development of the country and the encouragement of overseas investment.

INVESTMENT PROFILE

In 1990, the Belize government introduced their own International Business Companies Act. The act mirrors the IBC acts of the British Virgin Islands and the Bahamas. However, this IBC has various amendments aimed at competing with the Caribbean centers and is perhaps now one of the most modern International Business Companies Acts currently in existence that offers total tax exemption. A Belize IBC cannot, however, carry on business with Belize residents, own an interest in real property located in Belize, be a bank, an insurance or reinsurance company or conduct the business of providing registered office for companies.

Companies incorporated in other jurisdictions may transfer their registration to Belize to become IBCs. Conversely, IBCs may continue as companies incorporated under the laws of a jurisdiction outside Belize.

The IBC legislation permits complete anonymity because no details of either members or directors are required to be filed with the Registrar of IBCs. For added protection, bearer shares and corporate directors may be utilized. A unique feature of the Belizean IBC legislation is Part XI which provides for Public Investment Companies (PIC). These are substantial and established companies which are listed or have applied for listing on one of the major stock exchanges around the world. As such, they must therefore meet the stringent requirements of those exchanges. Part XI makes specific provision for such established companies to become PICs and then to use the more modem and flexible legislation contained in the IBC Act.

PICs have been created to promote overseas investment in Belize by granting additional tax and other concessions to the PIC and its subsidiaries, the latter often comprising operating companies in Belize.

TAXATION

Companies that do not qualify for International Business Company exemption status are subject to the normal company tax rate of 45 percent. Dividends of Belize-registered companies are deductible from income tax and are included in the chargeable income of the shareholder of the person receiving the dividend. Companies are not subject to capital gains tax, turnover tax or any other taxation. Individuals are subject to rates beginning at 5 percent for the first 7,000 Belize dollars ($3,500) increasing to 50 percent over 60,000 Belize dollars ($30,000).

BERMUDA

AT A GLANCE...

Capital
Hamilton

Commercial Center
Hamilton

Location
The islands of Bermuda are located approximately 600 miles off the east coast of the United States. There are seven main islands, all connected by bridges.

Climate
Bermuda has a semitropical climate with temperatures ranging from 50°F to 90°F.

Population
The population of Bermuda is 56,000.

Language
The official language of Bermuda is English.

Currency
The unit of currency is the Bermudian dollar.

Communications
Bermuda is highly accessible. Daily flights connect it with most major cities in the world. It is located at the crossroads of the shipping lanes between the United States, Canada, northern Europe and South America. Direct dialing, courier, telex and airmail services are excellent.

OVERVIEW

Bermuda is a prestigious offshore business center that attracts a very polished clientele. A tourist's delight, Bermuda has a moderate climate that is warmed by the Gulf Stream.

LEGAL SYSTEM

The legal tradition Bermuda derives from an ancient, pre-1612 British common law, modified by locally generated common law. The legal framework is three-tiered: magistrates courts, a supreme court and a court of appeals. As in most commonwealth countries, the ultimate court of appeals is the Queen's privy council in London.

GOVERNMENT

Bermuda is a self-governing crown colony and a fully independent commonwealth member. It has a governor appointed by the Queen. This official has larger responsibilities than his or her Bahamian counterpart. He or she handles foreign relations, security and the law enforcement department. All other affairs are monitored by the democratic institutions of the colony.

The legislature is bicameral with an appointed upper house and an elected lower house. The governor heads the cabinet.

INVESTMENT PROFILE

There are two basic types of companies recognized by Bermudian corporate legislation: local companies and exempt companies. Local companies are those formed by Bermudians for purposes of internal trade or Bermuda-based international trade—import to and export from Bermuda. Such companies have a minimum percentage of local stock ownership prescribed by law and are subject to strict exchange control. These companies have no guaranteed immunity against future taxes.

An exempt company is free of the first two restrictions and is given an official guarantee against the levying of future taxes for thirty years. However, an exempt company is restricted as follows:

1) It cannot buy, lease or sell land mortgages secured by land or bonds and debentures secured by land without special permission.
2) It cannot buy shares of local companies.
3) It cannot locally sell whatever it produces without special ad hoc permission. Incorporation is difficult in Bermuda. There is a

stiff maintenance fee ($2,000—$2,500) and a screening of incorporation applicants. There also are problems with immigration and work permits for aliens and renting a local office is difficult. Local companies pay a five percent payroll tax that does not apply to exempt companies. This, however, is a bad sign for a tax haven.

TAXATION

Great Britain gets no tax money from Bermuda. Thus, the high British taxes have no bearing on the tax situation in Bermuda. The self-governing nature of Bermuda means that any changes in the tax laws or other legislation must come from the local legislature.

Currently, Bermuda has no double-taxation treaties with any other countries.

BRITISH VIRGIN ISLANDS

AT A GLANCE...

Capital
Road Town

Commercial Center
Road Town (Tortola)

Location
The British Virgin Islands consist of 60 islands and cays having a total land area of 59 square miles. The islands are northwest of the United States Virgin Islands and are separated by a

channel. Puerto Rico is 60 miles to the west. Except for the Anegada, which is a flat, coral island with little soil, the islands are hilly.

Climate

The temperature ranges from 70° to 90°F.

Population

The largest and most heavily populated island is Tortola, which has about 9,000 inhabitants. The capital, Road Town, is on the southern shore near Sir Francis Drake Channel. Tortola is connected by a bridge to Beef Island. There are 3,000 inhabitants who reside on the other islands.

Language

The official and spoken language is English.

Currency

The unit of currency is the U.S. dollar.

Communications

There is an excellent daily service between the islands and the United States. Cruise ships call in weekly to the islands as well as freight carriers. There are excellent telephone, telex and fax facilities. Courier services are well represented on the islands (DHL, DLT and Federal Express).

OVERVIEW

The British Virgin Islands were discovered by Columbus who is said to have been so impressed by their large number that he named them "Las Virgenes" in honor of St. Ursula and her 11,000 attendant virgins. The islands are known for their superb beaches. There are no forests or rivers.

No exchange controls exist between the British Virgin Islands and the United States and confidentiality is considered very important. There are six main banks on the island and numbered accounts are unknown.

LEGAL SYSTEM

At the top of the court hierarchy is the West Indies Associated States supreme court, consisting of a high court of justice and a court of appeal. Lower courts are the court of summary jurisdiction and the magistrate's court.

The legal system is based upon English common law. There is no system of local government but the governor appoints a local officer for the islands of Angegada, Virgin Gorda and Jost Van Dyke.

GOVERNMENT

The British Virgin Islands is a stable, self-governed British crown colony under the 1967 constitution.

At present the British Virgin Islands is an internally self-governing colony with a ministerial system of government operating under a constitution adopted in 1967. The governor, appointed by the crown, remains responsible for defense and internal security, external affairs, the civil service, the administration of the courts and finance.

INVESTMENT PROFILE

There are three types of companies available in the British Virgin Islands: the International Business Company (IBC), the CAP 243 resident company and the CAP 243 non-resident company.

The IBC is one of the most modern corporate statutes currently in existence.

An IBC company, however, is restricted from doing business with British Virgin Island residents and owning property on the islands. An IBC can be incorporated with any name that is considered undesirable by the registrar. There must be a registered office in the British Virgin Islands, and there also must be a registered agent who must be either a lawyer, a solicitor, a chartered accountant or a licensed trust or management company.

The CAP 243 resident company is utilized exclusively for carrying on business in the British Virgin Islands and would qualify for treaty relief under the current taxation treaties. For domestic business, the company would pay 15 percent tax on its chargeable income.

The CAP 243 non-resident company is deemed to be non-resident for taxation purposes if the control and management of the affairs of the company are exercised outside the British Virgin Islands. These companies pay a flat license fee of U.S. $250 to the British Virgin Islands government and an annual return filing fee of U.S. $50. There is a requirement for two directors and a company secretary and the minimum number of shareholders is two. There is no requirement to file audited accounts.

TAXATION

A long-existing and popular treaty with the United States was terminated as of January 1, 1983 because officials of the two governments could not agree on a satisfactory settlement in the drawn-out negotiations of a new treaty. Under the extension still in effect, dividends arising in the territory may be subject to a 15-percent withholding tax and in most cases, there is no withholding on royalties, technical assistance fees and interest paid from the British Virgin Islands. The withholding tax on income paid by persons in a participating treaty country: A maximum of 15 percent for dividends, normal rates for interest and none for royalties.

There are no taxes on income, profit, sales, value added, withholding or capital gains.

THE CAYMAN ISLANDS

AT A GLANCE...

Capital
George Town

Commercial Center
George Town

Location
The Cayman Islands consist of a group of three islands in the Caribbean. The main island, Grand Cayman, is situated approximately 450 miles south of Florida. The three islands have a total area of 102 square miles with Grand Cayman having an area of 75 square miles.

Climate
The Cayman Islands have a tropical climate providing mild dry winters with temperatures between 65° and 75°F and warm summers with temperatures between 75° and 85°F.

Rainfall is light the months through November to April.

Population

The population of the three islands is approximately 26,000, the majority of which reside on Grand Cayman.

Language

The official and spoken language is English.

Currency

The unit of currency is the Cayman Islands dollar.

Communications

There are excellent telephone, fax and telex facilities with direct dialing to and from the rest of the world. Miami is one hour away by air. The islands also have direct air links with New York, Costa Rica, Atlanta, Tampa, Houston and Jamaica, as well as being a popular cruise ship stop.

OVERVIEW

The economy of the islands is strong and enjoys full employment with most of the revenue being derived from the financial services sector and tourism.

Being a tax haven is a tradition based on British rule. Here, however, the tradition is bolstered by a legend. In 1778, the islanders heroically saved, from tragic death at sea, a British royal prince, his mentor and an admiral. King George III gratefully granted the islanders eternal tax exemption.

The Cayman Islands' government is very supportive of the tax haven industry because it is a major factor in local economic growth.

LEGAL SYSTEM

The Cayman Islands have their own courts of law with the rights of appeal to the Cayman Court of appeal and then ultimately to the privy council in England. Cayman Islands' law is based on English common law.

GOVERNMENT

The Cayman Islands are a British colony and therefore under the jurisdiction of the United Kingdom. Parliament at Westminster retains the right to legislate. The islands have a governor who is appointed by the queen.

The governor heads the Cayman Islands' government and is responsible for the civil service, defense, the police department and external affairs. There is a legislative assembly consisting of 12 elected members as well as the financial secretary, the attorney general and the administrative secretary.

INVESTMENT PROFILE

There are three basic types of Cayman Islands companies: Ordinary resident companies, ordinary non-resident companies and exempt companies. Exempt companies are primarily used by non-residents for international tax-planning purposes.

An exempt company may not carry on a business in the Cayman Islands other than its international activities. It may not own real property or transact any business with residents of the Cayman Islands. The company may support a registered office address and engage the services of a management company, an accountant and/or solicitor to attend to administration, compliance and other statutory duties.

Exempt companies are normally incorporated with an authorized share capital of U.S. $900,000 or its foreign currency equivalent. This is the maximum authorized share capital for the minimum government fees. Exempt companies can issue no par value shares, or bearer shares. In the case of bearer shares, these must be fully paid up.

All Cayman Island companies must maintain a registered office address in the Cayman Islands.

TAXATION

The Cayman Islands are a pure tax haven with no direct taxation being levied on residents or corporations. There are no capital gains, inheritance or gift taxes although there is stamp duty on real property of 7.5 percent on transfer and one percent on mortgages.

No double taxation treaties exist since there are no taxes. The Caymans have signed an exchange of information agreement with the United States.

COOK ISLANDS

AT A GLANCE...

Capital
Avarua (Rarotonga)

Commercial Center
Avarua

Location
The Cook Islands are comprised of 15 islands in the South Pacific ocean between Tahiti in the east and Samoa

and Tonga in the west. The main island is Rarotonga.

Climate
The climate is similar to New Zealand.

Population
The total population of the Cook Islands is 19,000, with approximately half the populace living on Rarotonga.

Language
The official language is English although Maori is widely spoken as well.

Currency
New Zealand currency is used in the islands. Exchange controls exist only on certain dealings designated in New Zealand dollars. There are no local restrictions on the movement of funds to or from the Cook Islands in other currencies, and funds may be held and business transacted in the Cook Islands in any currency. Because New Zealand has now removed its exchange controls, international entities have no restraints on dealings in New Zealand dollars.

Communications
Rarotonga has a continuous international telephone, telex and facsimile service via satellite. Direct dialing to Rarotonga is available from most countries. There also are good international postal and courier services.

OVERVIEW

The government has reaffirmed continuing support and encouragement for the development of Rarotonga as a financial center. The Cook Islands is growing in international stature. The islands are a member of the South Pacific Forum, the Economic Commission for Asia and the Pacific and the Asian Development Bank.

LEGAL SYSTEM

The court of the Cook Islands, established in 1964, is the superior court of the islands. The legal system is based on the principles of English common law and equity.

Appeals are made to the Cook Islands court of appeal (which must include a current or former judge of the court of appeal of New Zealand) and to the privy council in England.

GOVERNMENT

Great Britain proclaimed a protectorate over the Cook Islands in 1888 and in 1901, the islands were ceded to New Zealand. The Cook Islands became fully self-governing in 1965 under the Cook Islands Constitution Act of 1964 which gave the islands a Westminster-model constitution. The islands have two main political parties.

INVESTMENT PROFILE

The two major banks in the Cook Islands are ANZ and Westpac Banking Corporation Limited. International companies can be incorporated if its shareholders are not residents of the Cook Islands. However, a trustee company registered under the Trustee Companies Act of 1981-1982, may hold shares in an international company and may be the sole shareholder.

There are no minimum capital requirements, and shares may be of no par value. Shares may be designated in all major currencies and bearer shares may be issued. Registered shares that have been fully paid may be exchanged for bearer shares unless this is prohibited by its articles of association.

An international company may be incorporated for any lawful purpose, other than that of a trustee company, but shall not carry on the business of banking or insurance unless licensed under the relevant act. An international company cannot carry on business in the Cook Islands unless it is registered under the Development Investment Act of 1977.

Cook Islands' legislation permits great flexibility through provisions which enable a company to transfer its domicile. The International Companies Act permits companies incorporated in other jurisdictions to transfer their registration to the Cook Islands as international companies. International companies may transfer their registration to other jurisdictions.

Principals or promoters of international companies may remain anonymous. Anonymity is further guaranteed by laws that impose penal sanctions on any person who discloses information derived from an inspection of the records of an international company. The documents lodged with the Registrar of International Companies are only available for inspection by directors, members and debenture holders. Court proceedings relating to the rights or obligations of officers or members or debenture holders must be heard in camera, unless the court orders otherwise.

A foreign company incorporated outside the Cook Islands may register under the International Companies Act 1981-82 (if it has a place of business or is carrying on business within the Cook Islands) or under the Companies Act of 1970-71. Registration under either act does not exempt a foreign company from compliance with the requirements of registration under the Development Investment Act if it is a "foreign enterprise," as defined under that Act.

TAXATION

The regulation of companies in the Cook Islands and their status is determined by whether they seek registration as domestic companies under the Cook Islands Companies Act of 1981-82.

Entities established within the offshore jurisdiction are exempt under the International Companies Act of 1981-1982 from any form of taxation, including stamp duties, capital gains tax, capital issue tax and withholding tax. The legislation also provides such entities with a guarantee that the Crown will not compulsorily acquire or expropriate their property situated in the Cook Islands except as defined by law. The Cook Islands are not a party to any double taxation treaty.

CYPRUS

AT A GLANCE...

Capital
Nicosia

Commercial Center
Nicosia

Location
Cyprus is located at the northeastern end of the Mediterranean Sea at the crossroads of Europe and Africa and lies south of Turkey, west of Syria, north of Egypt and southeast of Athens.

Climate
Cyprus has a pleasant climate with dry, hot summers and mild winters. The rainy season is confined to the period between November and March.

Population
The population is approximately 700,000.

Language
Greek and Turkish are the official languages of Cyprus (Turkish being used only in the occupied north part of Cyprus). English is widely spoken and understood, particularly in commercial and government sectors.

Currency
The unit of currency is the pound.

Communications
Larnaca International Airport replaced Nicosia as the main international airport in 1975 and a second, smaller international airport near Paphos became operational in late 1985. There are frequent air connections to many international destinations.
Cyprus has good telecommunication links with the rest of the world. Eighty-five countries can be reached on a direct-dialing system. There also are excellent postal and courier services.

OVERVIEW

Cyprus is an island country in the Eastern Mediterranean. It was formerly a British colony, but since 1960, it has been independent. It is a member of the United Nations, the Council of Europe and the Commonwealth, and has established a relationship with the European Community that will eventually lead to a full customs union (although not to full membership in the European Community).

Cyprus maintains politically and economically viable relations with the Arab nations, as well as Eastern European countries. Its ties to Britain and Greece are close. The northern portion of the island has been occupied by Turkish forces and declared independence. This is not thought of as a deterrent to its tax haven uses.

LEGAL SYSTEM

The legal system is based on the same principles applicable in the United Kingdom and all statutes regulating business matters and procedure are based on English law. Most laws are officially translated into English.

Criminal jurisdiction is in six district courts for minor offenses and in six assize courts for more serious crimes. All appeals are heard by the supreme court which pronounces final judgment.

GOVERNMENT

Cyprus became an independent republic in 1960. The political system is modeled on western democracies in which individual rights are respected and private enterprise is given every opportunity to develop. Under its constitution, Cyprus has a presidential system of government. The president is the head of state and is elected for a five-year term of office.

The executive arm of the government is the council of ministers, and the members are appointed by the president. The ministers are responsible for the administration of matters within their domain and for the implementation of legislation. Legislative power is in the hands of the house of representatives.

INVESTMENT PROFILE

As a result of its relationship with Great Britain, Cyprus is a common law country with its company laws patterned after Great Britain. The costs for organizing and maintaining a Cyprus company are based on Cyprus internal costs and are quite low.

Cyprus is popular for shipping companies, and there are two ways of using Cyprus for other companies. One is the Cyprus-registered company, which if owned by non-residents and dealing only with foreign business, pays tax at a tenth of the normal corporate tax rate (i.e. 4.25 percent). The branch office of a foreign company pays no Cyprus income tax on its non-resident business.

The branch cannot use the Cyprus double-taxation agreements, although the Cyprus registered company can, because the latter is a resident of Cyprus. For tax purposes, the offshore company may be a holding company, a finance company, an investment company, an insurance company or a management company.

Every company must maintain a registered office address in Cyprus, the address of which is determined by filing a return with the Registrar of Companies at the time of registration.

An offshore Cyprus company must have at least one director. Every company must have a company secretary appointed by the directors. The company secretary may be either a person or a company, but they must be a Cyprus resident.

TAXATION

Companies registered in Cyprus, whose shares are directly or indirectly owned by foreigners and whose income is derived from sources outside Cyprus, qualify as 'offshore companies.' These companies pay 4.25 percent tax in Cyprus. This applies irrespective of the place of management and control of the company. Shareholders receiving dividends from offshore companies are not subject to any further tax on dividends.

Cyprus has an excellent network of double-taxation agreements, most of which are comprehensive and follow the OECD model. Under these agreements opportunities exist to obtain income from contracting states which has either no tax at all or has been subject to tax at reduced rates in those contracting states.

GIBRALTAR

AT A GLANCE...

Capital
Gibraltar

Commercial Center
Gibraltar

Location
Gibraltar is a peninsula at the southern tip of Spain. It is adjacent to Africa but within Europe and has an historically strategic position at the junction of the Atlantic and the Mediterranean.

Climate
Warm, dry summers and mild winters characterize the climate of Gibraltar.

Population
The population is approximately 30,000, although a substantial number of the working population commute daily from homes nearby in Spain.

Language
The official and spoken language is English, although Spanish is spoken widely.

Currency
While Gibraltar issues its own currency, money of the United Kingdom also is considered to be legal tender.

Communications
Gibraltar possesses the support system needed by modern companies. A new telephone system has been in operation since 1990. The jurisdiction boasts excellent telecommunications and postal facilities, and also features daily air service to Europe and the rest of the world. Its banking facilities are excellent and are expected to improve as Gibraltar continues to attract international banks.

OVERVIEW

Gibraltar is a member of the European Community and enjoys a special status within the community. It is exempted from the common customs tariff, the common agricultural policy and the value-added tax. Gibraltar is politically stable, and the current government was recently re-elected by a large majority. The government actively promotes Gibraltar as a first-class international financial center.

LEGAL SYSTEM

While Gibraltar has an independent legal system, it is a common law jurisdiction based on English law with variations introduced by local ordinances. There is an independent judiciary with lower courts, court of first instance and a supreme court. The ultimate court of appeals is the privy council in England.

GOVERNMENT

Gibraltar is a British dependent territory with internal self-government. It has its own elected house of assembly which legislates on domestic matters. The United Kingdom is responsible for defense, foreign affairs, financial stability and internal security.

INVESTMENT PROFILE

Gibraltar is rapidly growing as an offshore center. Although it is a low-cost jurisdiction, it has relatively high taxes for residents. Its standard income tax rate for individuals is 30 percent with the tax rising to a maximum of 50 percent, while its income tax rate for resident companies is 35 percent. Still, Gibraltar offers three types of companies that provide

important tax advantages: The non-resident company, the exempt company and the qualifying company.

The non-resident company is incorporated in Gibraltar but is managed by directors residing outside the jurisdiction. If the company does not derive its income from within Gibraltar, it is outside the scope of Gibraltarian income tax. Unlike other jurisdictions which charge an annual company registration tax or non-resident company duty, Gibraltar does not apply flat rate fees against non-resident companies.

A Gibraltar company may apply for exempt status. This is done after incorporation and takes between 10 and 14 days, depending on the company and the details of the application. Once obtained, the company receives an exemption certificate that is valid for 25 years and grants a full exemption from income tax and estate duty in Gibraltar. The exempt company pays a flat annual duty. The following must be met before exempt status is granted:

- Written references from a professional
- Statement on the proposed activities of the company
- A guarantee that business be conducted only with other exempt companies
- No changes in beneficial ownership, shareholders or objectives unless approved by the Gibraltar authorities
- No shares held by a Gibraltarian or a resident of Gibraltar
- Annual tax paid in two equal installments

Qualifying companies were created

in the Income Tax (Amendment) Ordinance of 1983 for situations where the authorities of a foreign country require proof that a percentage of tax on profits has already been paid in Gibraltar. The tax rates for Gibraltar are 2 percent for income not paid to Gibraltar and 17 percent for income paid to Gibraltar. To obtain a qualifying status, the same requirements for the exempt company apply plus the following:

- A one-time fee of 250 pounds
- A minimum paid-up share capital of 1,000 pounds
- A deposit of 1,000 pounds

TAXATION

Gibraltar offers considerable opportunities to both individuals and companies wishing to minimize tax liability. Income tax is levied under the Income Tax Ordinance of 1952 (as amended) and the rate of taxation is between 20 to 50 percent for resident individuals and companies. Non-residents are only liable for Gibraltar income tax when the income originates in Gibraltar. The exemption to this rule: income earned on bank accounts.

Gibraltar does not currently have any double-taxation treaties. Gibraltar tax authorities do not exchange or disclose information with or to any other tax authorities. There is no capital gains tax in Gibraltar.

GREECE

AT A GLANCE...

Capital
Athens

Commercial Center
Athens

Location
Greece is the southernmost country on the Balkan peninsula in southern Europe.

Climate
Greece has mild winters and hot, humid summers.

Population
The population is approximately 10.5 million.

Language
The official language is Greek and the business community speaks English.

Currency
The unit of currency is the drachma.

Communications
Many major airlines serve Greece and the country has a good communications system and an excellent postal service.

OVERVIEW

Greece's tax haven laws have been responsible for the sound economic growth of the nation. Any foreign commercial or industrial company that establishes a regional office in Greece receives total exemption from income tax as well as other significant tax benefits.

LEGAL SYSTEM

The special supreme tribunal is the highest court in Greece. The court rules on the constitutionality of laws and decides election and referendum disputes. The regular court system is made up of the administrative, civil, criminal, appellate and supreme courts.

GOVERNMENT

In 1974, Greece overthrew a military dictatorship and now has a republic-style government. Ceremonial executive power is held by the president. The premier heads the government and is responsible to a 300-member unicameral parliament.

INVESTMENT PROFILE

The establishment of a Greek regional office is subject to the approval of the minister of coordination and is contingent upon granting power of attorney to a permanent Greek resident who will act as the foreign company's legal representative.

To effect the power of attorney, a statement must be written in the home country stating that the party giving the power of attorney is a duly constituted corporation. The foreign parent company also may be asked by the minister of coordination to file a copy of the annual balance sheet as well as a profit-and-loss statement.

TAXATION

A regional office that derives no income from Greece receives the following benefits:
- Exemption from all Greek taxes
- Exemption from income tax on earnings of foreign personnel
- Exemption from all customs duties, stamp duties, import taxes and luxury taxes on items imported to equip the regional office
- Exemption from duties on the importation of household items by the firm's foreign personnel
- Exemption from any requirement to keep books in the Greek language
- Exemption from requesting the approval of the post office to post registered letters abroad
- Exemption from any export-import duties relating to samples of advertising material by the regional firm
- Exemption from tax on interest received from deposits in Greek banks from government bonds
- Exemption for certain specified enterprises from a tax on the profits from sale of securities
- Exemption from any tax on interest from loans granted by foreign banks or firms to certain Greek entities
- Exemption from duties on the conversion of bond or preference shares of corporations and on the replacement of share or bond certificates
- Two-year work permits for foreign personnel with extensions obtainable

GUERNSEY

AT A GLANCE...

Capital
St. Peter Port

Commercial Center
St. Peter Port

Location
Guernsey is the second largest of the Channel Islands and is located in the English Channel off the northwest coast of France. It is important to

distinguish between the island of Guernsey and the "Bailiwick" of Guernsey.

The island of Guernsey consists of Guernsey Island and the Lihou, Herm and Jethou Islands. The Bailiwick of Guernsey consists of the island of Guernsey, Alderney and the Fief of Sark.

Climate

The climate of Guernsey is generally warmer than that of the south coast of England.

Population

The population is 55,000 and like Jersey, Guernsey adopts an extremely complicated system of residential-housing control primarily to prevent further growth in the population and to protect the interests of Guernsey indigenous residents.

Language

English is now the official language throughout Guernsey having replaced French in commercial and legal matters during the early part of the 20th century.

Currency

Although British currency is used in Guernsey, English and local money circulates. In addition, Jersey currency circulates in Guernsey. Guernsey money circulates in Jersey, and even French money is sometimes accepted and exchanged informally.

Communications

Telephone, telefax and postal services are excellent, and most of the international courier companies operate fast and efficient services. Air service, particularly to and from the United Kingdom and continental Europe, is excellent.

OVERVIEW

The economy of Guernsey is predominantly based on tourism, farming and financial services. In recent years, however, farming has been declining as the financial services sector has become increasingly important.

LEGAL SYSTEM

As well as its own parliament, Guernsey has its own legal system. The Bailiff presides over the royal court as well as over the states. There is a right of appeal from the royal court to the Guernsey court of appeal and thereafter to the privy council. The majority of recent Guernsey legislation is derived from the United Kingdom but there are significant differences, particularly in areas such as inheritance and company law.

GOVERNMENT

Since 1204, Guernsey's sovereign has been the English monarch. The Bailiwick forms part of the British Isles but is not part of the United Kingdom. Although constitutionally it owes allegiance to the English crown (represented in the Bailiwick by the Queen's lieutenant governor), it has its own separate legislature. The United Kingdom remains responsible for the island's defense and foreign affairs, and the crown the privy council has overriding control over legislation in specific areas.

It has no right to impose legislation in relation to domestic and, more particularly, fiscal matters in the Bailiwick without the consent of Guernsey.

INVESTMENT PROFILE

Although perhaps not as well known as many of the other offshore havens, Guernsey offers significant advantages for investors including stability, a comparatively free economic climate and favorable tax laws for companies. English common law encourages banks and their personnel to maintain secrecy. There also is privilege against disclosure.

There is no distinction between private or public companies although public companies who offer shares to the public must allot the minimum subscription and file a declaration. For tax purposes, there is a distinction between resident companies and exempt companies. To qualify as an exempt company, a declaration has to be filed with the administrator of income tax confirming that:

- No shares of the company are beneficially owned by a resident of Guernsey.
- No income will arise from Guernsey sources other than Guernsey bank interest.

The formation of an exempt company is subject to prior consent from the Financial Services Commission and the following information must be supplied:

- The names and addresses of the ultimate beneficial owners
- Character references relating to the ultimate beneficial owners
- The objectives of the company
- Whether or not the company will be used to avoid an existing United

Kingdom tax liability
- The place where the central management and control is to be exercised
- The authorized and intended share capital

TAXATION

It is the policy of the Guernsey Islands' treasury to maintain a rate of direct taxation at 20 percent. The Guernsey tax year runs from January 1 to December 31. Resident Guernsey individuals and companies are therefore taxed at 20 percent on chargeable income. There are no wealth, capital gains or inheritance taxes with the exception of short-term capital gains taxes that apply to property.

A non-resident company is managed, controlled and conducts its trade outside of Guernsey. Such companies are subject to corporation tax at the rate of 500 pounds per year, which is due each January. The corporation tax is payable in advance, and the first payment is due at incorporation. The payment is then levied pro rata during the year of incorporation from the date of incorporation to December 31.

HONG KONG

AT A GLANCE...

Capital
Victoria

Commercial Center
Victoria

Location
Hong Kong is on the southeast tip of China and consists of a large number of

islands and a part of the Chinese mainland totaling approximately 400 square miles. The principal areas are the Island of Hong, Kowloon and the New Territories. These areas were ceded to Britain in perpetuity in 1842 under the treaty of Nankinu. In 1898, the new territories were leased by Britain from China for a period of 99 years and includes all the land north of Boundary Street in Kowloon to the border with China as well as 235 small islands.

Climate

Hong Kong's subtropical and monsoonal climate produces dry, cool winters with an average temperature of 59°F. Summers are hot and rainy with an average temperature of 82°F. Humidity runs high.

Population

The population is currently six million. Hong Kong is one of the most densely populated areas in the world.

Language

The official languages are English and Chinese with English being used in the commercial and political context and Cantonese Chinese used widely in industry and domestic trade.

Currency

The unit of currency is the Hong Kong dollar.

Communications

Hong Kong is a prominent trade and manufacturing center with superb transportation and communication facilities. Major airlines connect Hong Kong by frequent flights to every major city in the world. The British civil service tradition, coupled with the pressures of demand, makes Hong Kong's airmail, telex and international telephone and cable services highly efficient, regular and reliable.

OVERVIEW

Hong Kong is the leading southeast Asian center for both finance and commerce and ranks as the world's third largest financial center after New York and London. There are more than 160 licensed banks with 128 foreign banks having representative offices in Hong Kong and a further 225 licensed deposit-taking finance companies.

LEGAL SYSTEM

The judiciary operates independently under the direction of the chief justice. Hong Kong's legal system is based on the principles of England as they existed in equity and the statutes of England as they existed in 1843. There has been some modification by the United Kingdom parliament and the Hong Kong legislature.

GOVERNMENT

Hong Kong has been a British crown colony since 1842. The governor, appointed by the Queen, presides over the Hong Kong government.

In 1984, an agreement was made on the future of Hong Kong between the British and Chinese governments. On July 1, 1997, all of Hong Kong became a special administrative region of China. For 50 years thereafter, the following will remain unaltered:

- A local government will continue with full authority in executive, legislative and judicial matters.

- The legal, social and economic systems remain in force.
- All forms of property, including inheritance and ownership by non-residents, will be respected.
- The current economic position, including the financial markets and the Hong Kong dollar, will continue.
- The financial system will remain independent, and China will not seek to raise any taxes in Hong Kong.
- Hong Kong will remain independent for customs purposes.
- Crown land leases may be granted for up to 50 years after 1997.
- The free port will remain.

INVESTMENT PROFILE

Company formation in Hong Kong follows the usual British pattern. A memorandum and articles of association are required, and they must include the standard information. All these requirements are purely formalities, because nominees can be used for everything.

Annual maintenance of a corporation involves annual auditing signed by a chartered accountant and submitted to all shareholders with a copy to the government. The government charges and annual maintenance fees are low. The initial expenses of incorporation, articles of association and stock certificates are approximately U.S. $500, and annual maintenance is about U.S. $500.

Incorporation takes up to a month to accomplish. It can be done with complete privacy through nominee

shareholders. There is no legal requirement that ultimate beneficiary owners be disclosed.

TAXATION

Hong Kong income tax is taken from income that has its source in Hong Kong rather than a tax based on residence. Hong Kong does not, therefore, impose tax on non-Hong Kong source income even when remitted to Hong Kong. Consequently, if a Hong Kong company's trading or business activities are based outside Hong Kong, no tax will be levied.

Hong Kong companies with Hong Kong source income currently pay a 16.5 percent tax on profits. For individuals, the maximum rate of taxation on income is 15 percent.

IRELAND

AT A GLANCE...

Capital
Dublin

Commercial Center
Dublin

Location
Ireland is located to the west of Great Britain and is separated from Great Britain by the Irish Sea.

Climate
The climate is mild, though often rainy and damp, ranging from 40°F in the winter to 60°F in the summer.

Population
Ireland has a population of approximately five million.

Language

The English language is the official business and commercial language. However, there are many areas such as the Aran Islands, Connemara, Glaway and Cork where Irish Gaelic is spoken.

Currency

The currency of Ireland is the Irish pound.

Communications

There are regularly scheduled flights to all major European airports as well as freight and ferry services available to Great Britain and France. Ireland has modern all-digital telecommunications facilities with direct-dial capability to 160 countries worldwide.

OVERVIEW

Ireland offers foreign entrepreneurs the benefits of an English-speaking work force, labor costs that are only 60 to 70 percent of U.S. levels and a 10-percent ceiling on taxes and cash grants.

One-stop shopping spares prospective investors the long-winded dealings with local authorities that can make foreign investment difficult. A considerable number of large multinational companies have taken advantage of the benefits of setting up Irish subsidiaries These incentives are for both small and large companies. The average foreign company in Ireland employs 40 to 50 workers.

LEGAL SYSTEM

The Republic of Ireland is a common-law jurisdiction. The legal system is similar to that of the United Kingdom, Australia and the United States. The members of the judiciary are appointed by the government. However, once appointed, their independence from the executive arm of government is guaranteed by the Irish constitution.

GOVERNMENT

The Republic of Ireland is a parliamentary democracy with a written constitution. Northern Ireland remains an integral part of the United Kingdom. The parliament is known as Dail Eireann and has 166 members. The senate is known as Seanad Eireann and functions in a similar manner to the House of Lords in the United Kingdom. The Republic of Ireland is a full member of the European Community.

INVESTMENT PROFILE

Since the 1970s the Irish government has pursued an aggressive foreign-investment program. But because of its participation in the Treaty of Rome, which governs relations between members of the European Community, Ireland is not a pure tax haven. However, to encourage foreign entrepreneurs to set up businesses in Ireland, the government created the Irish Development Authority (IDA).

The IDA has broad powers to approve applications and make grants to prospective employers. To start up a business and win special grants for creating jobs, entrepreneurs should contact the nearest IDA office. Local IDA officials will be available to provide back-up assistance.

To qualify for IDA incentives, a company must be engaged either in manufacturing or in international services. To qualify for IDA tax breaks and capital grants, a financial company must employ a minimum of 10 people. There is a minimum size for manufacturing companies.

The Irish parliament passed a law extending to the year 2010 the maximum corporate tax rate of 10 percent on foreign investments. Thus, companies investing now can look forward to tax relief.

TAXATION

Corporation tax is payable by resident companies at a rate of 40 percent on all income and capital gains, and non-resident company status is a feature of taxation law. To obtain and maintain non-resident status, the ownership and center of management of a non-resident company should be foreign-based and the company should not derive any income from the Republic of Ireland. All companies must file accounts and an annual return with the registry. Non-resident companies do not, however, need to file accounts with the tax authority although the tax authority reserves the right to call for accounts if it so wishes.

ISLE OF MAN

AT A GLANCE...

Capital
Douglas

Commercial Center
Douglas

Location
The Isle of Man is located on the Irish Sea and is close to England, Scotland and Ireland.

Climate
The island has a temperate climate and, due to the influence of the sea, rarely experiences extremes of either heat or cold. The sunniest months are April, May and June.

Population
The population is approximately 70,000.

Language
The official and spoken language is English. However, owing to the island's Celtic origins, it also has its own Gaelic language.

Currency
The monetary units are the British pound, Scottish currency and the Isle of Man pound note.

Communications
The Isle of Man is served by Ronaldsway Airport in the south of the island some eight miles from Douglas. There are regular services on at least a daily basis to most major cities in Great Britain. The island has some 500 miles of roads connecting all the major centers of population. Telephone, telefax and telex services are excellent. The postal services work in very close liaison with those in the United Kingdom. International courier services are available with connections via Heathrow.

OVERVIEW

The Isle of Man, confronted with a decline in its two principal sources of income, agriculture and tourism, now places greater reliance upon industrial investment and its financial center activities which now contribute more than 30 percent to the gross national product.

The Isle of Man is the only low-tax financial center in Europe that actively encourages new residents.

More than 50 licensed banks, including many international banks, are present on the island. Their services are comprehensive, discreet and confidential, comparing favorably with the banking sectors of Switzerland and Liechtenstein. In addition to banking, high-caliber legal, accounting, insurance and other financial services are available on the island.

LEGAL SYSTEM

Isle of Man law is based on English common law and much of the civil-law legislation is modeled on United Kingdom acts of parliament. The island has its own courts and the heads of the judicial system are known as "deemsters." Advocates of the Manx Bar have the combined role of both solicitors and barristers and are able to appear in both the lower and higher courts. The ultimate court of appeals is the English privy council.

GOVERNMENT

The Isle of Man is a dependency of the British crown. However, it has never been part of the United Kingdom or its colonies. The government dates back to Viking times, and its own independent parliament, Tynwalk, has existed for more than 1,000 years. While the Isle of Man is tied closely to the United Kingdom, which insures the island's defense and presides over international affairs, Tynwald is responsible for all aspects of domestic legislation, including taxation.

INVESTMENT PROFILE

To support the government's decision to become a leading European tax haven for offshore funds, the Isle of Man subsequently adopted an industrial aid and incentive package which is considered to be one of the most attractive in the western world.

Isle of Man resident and non-resident companies can engage in any activity worldwide, but exempt companies can only be used for insurance, shipping, property investment, investment holding, commodity dealing or the holding of patents, royalties, copyrights, licenses and trademarks. The Isle of Man offers several investment vehicles, each providing its own advantages:

- Exempt companies—If granted exempt status, a company's offshore income and dividends will be exempt from island income tax.
- Non-resident companies—A company may be incorporated on the island but remain non-resident. As such, it will be exempt from income tax, although it will have to pay an annual non-resident duty. A non-resident company could be used for protecting assets owned by an individual resident in another country.
- Trading companies—Various companies in the manufacturing and service sectors enjoy

advantages because of the island's relationship with the EC, existence of a freeport, low costs, tax structure and a generous range of grants and incentives offered by the island's government.

- Banks—As the island's government continues to encourage foreign investment, it is likely that the growth of the financial sector will continue, adding many opportunities for banks.

TAXATION

Apart from a limited treaty with the United Kingdom, the Isle of Man is not party to any double-taxation treaties. Isle of Man residents pay income tax only on their worldwide income at a rate of 15 percent for the first chargeable amount and 20 percent thereafter.

Along with these many advantages, the Isle of Man offers an attractive tax structure. The major features are well worth noting:

- No capital-gains tax
- No estate or inheritance taxes
- Tax-free holidays for industry
- Exempt offshore
- Value-added tax at 15 percent

JERSEY

AT A GLANCE...

Capital
St. Helier

Commercial Center
St. Helier

Location
Jersey is the largest of the Channel Islands which are located off the northwest coast of France near the Cherbourg peninsula. Jersey is approximately one-hundred miles south of England and fourteen miles from France.

Climate
Jersey benefits from the influence of the Gulf Stream. It is generally warmer than the south coast of England.

Population
The population is approximately 83,000 and effective immigration controls exist to restrict future growth through the Housing Jersey Law of 1949 which controls the sales and leases of land.

Language
English is used in all aspects of the island's financial and commercial activities.

Currency
The currency of the island is the pound sterling, and while the States of Jersey issue their own currency notes, these are legal tender only within the island and are easily converted to sterling as necessary.

Communications
Jersey enjoys excellent telecommunications with the rest of the world because it is part of the United Kingdom's STD network. Courier services operate in Jersey and are routed via London.

Jersey relies upon sea transportation for the importation of the majority of the goods and materials needed for the economy.

OVERVIEW

While the financial-services sector provides Jersey's main source of income, the tourist industry continues to represent 40 percent of the island's GDP. Amendments to the Income Tax Law, effective from 1989, add to Jersey's appeal as a possible tax haven.

One of the most significant provisions of these amendments is the creation of the "exempt company." An exempt company is treated as non-resident and thus gains considerable tax advantages.

LEGAL SYSTEM

The judiciary consists of the petty debts court, the royal court of Jersey, the court of appeals and the privy council. It has an independent system of law distinct from that of both England and the other Channel Islands. The sources of law in Jersey are:

- Common Law—This derives mainly from the ancient customary law of the Duchy of Normandy and applies in particular to real property, hypothecation and succession.
- Legislation—New legislation usually follows English legislation in a form adapted to the particular needs of the island.
- Judicial decision—Where no clear precedent can be drawn from the laws of Jersey, the Jersey courts have regard not only to the law of Normandy but also to the law of England.

GOVERNMENT

The constitutional relationship between the Channel Islands and the United Kingdom is unique. The respective legislative assemblies have the exclusive right to legislate on matters of domestic concern to the islands (including taxation) while the United Kingdom home office is responsible for the island's external affairs.

INVESTMENT PROFILE

While there is no legislation on bank secrecy or secrecy of information, it is possible, through the use of a numbered account, to restrict the identification of an account holder to senior bank officers.

It is felt that a legal duty exists to maintain secrecy which arises out of the implied contract between professional advisors. Only through law or by order of the royal court is information subject to disclosure. Exchange of information is provided for by two double-taxation agreements, one with the United Kingdom and one with Guernsey.

Investors who wish to form a company in Jersey have several advantages. A company incorporated and controlled in Jersey pays a 20-percent income tax. Although the formation of a company for Jersey income-tax purposes requires a declaration of the beneficial ownership of shares, nominee shareholders are not disclosed to the company registry, and the name of the beneficial owner will not appear in any search.

TAXATION

The major tax in Jersey is on income. The law relating to income tax can be found in the Jersey Law of 1961 as amended. There are no wealth, capital gains, gifts or inheritance taxes and the current rate of income tax is 20 percent for resident individuals and corporations.

JORDAN

AT A GLANCE...

Capital
Amman

Commercial Center
Amman

Location
Jordan is bordered on the west by Israel and the Dead Sea, on the north by Syria, on the east by Iraq and on the south by Saudi Arabia.

Climate
Average summer temperatures in Jordan range from 64°F to 100°F. Winters are mild with temperatures averaging 50°F.

Population
The population is approximately 3.6 million.

Language
The official language is Arabic.

Currency
The unit of currency is the Jordanian dinar.

Communications
Communications are excellent. Jordan has excellent highways and air-service links to Europe and neighboring countries. A direct-dial system has been installed for calls to the United States and Europe.

OVERVIEW

Jordan is a small Arab nation strategically located near the Red Sea,

Mediterranean Sea and the Arab markets of the Middle East. To encourage international business to open regional offices, Jordan has introduced special tax-haven legislation. Now that Beirut is no longer available as a regional headquarters for international trading companies, Jordan may well achieve the status of a major tax haven and regional headquarters location for trade in the Middle East.

LEGAL SYSTEM

The legal system consists of civil, religious and special courts. The civil courts handle commercial, criminal and civil cases. The religious courts handle personal and family matters. The special courts handle technical and legal matters. The king appoints all judges.

GOVERNMENT

Jordan is a constitutional monarchy with a bicameral parliament.

INVESTMENT PROFILE

Jordan's tax-exemption law for foreign companies, together with the many other concessions and incentives that are offered, should create a healthy international business scene in the Arab kingdom.

Jordanian law is called the Foreign Companies Registration law. Under the law, a foreign company can establish a Jordan-based branch for engaging in business outside Jordan. The fact that the law does not permit the foreign company to conduct business in Jordan should present no obstacle to the enterprising firm that can use such a strategic location to reach gulf markets.

TAXATION

A company registering under Jordan's Foreign Companies Registration law will find itself in line for many tax benefits including:

- Total exemption from income and social security taxes.
- Exemption from registration with the Chamber of Commerce and from the payment of registration taxes.
- Exemption from customs duties on the furnishing and equipment for the Jordan branch office.
- Exemption from duties on the importation of commercial samples.

Jordan also grants non-resident exchange control status to the regional office so that it may maintain bank accounts in foreign currency.

LIBERIA

AT A GLANCE...

Capital
Monrovia

Commercial Center
Monrovia

Location
Liberia is located on the west coast of Africa between Sierra Leone, Guinea and the Ivory Coast.

Climate
The Liberian climate is tropical with a rainy season from May to October and a dry season from November to April.

Population
The Liberian population is approximately 2.5 million, 300,000 of which live in the capital Monrovia.

Language
English is the official language of Liberia although there are 16 indigenous languages which are used throughout the country.

Currency
The unit of currency is the Liberian dollar.

Communications
Direct dialing and telex services are available. Monrovia and the newer port of Buchanan are among the most modern ports on the west coast of Africa and are regular ports of call for major steamship lines operating between Europe, the United States and the Far East. There are excellent direct flights from both Europe and the United States. Roberts International Airport is located on the outskirts of Monrovia. Airmail services are good, and the international courier services are well established in the country.

OVERVIEW

Liberia is one of the oldest tax havens, and perhaps somewhat unique for the simple fact that it has no infrastructure and the tax-haven clientele never goes there. The civil war of recent years has not affected the use of Liberia as a tax haven. Liberia is in the business of registering corporations and ships. There are no other services offered. There is no infrastructure of local attorneys or accountants. All contact is carried out with Liberian correspondent offices in New York or Zurich.

LEGAL SYSTEM

Liberian law was based on that of the United States and can be found in the Liberian Code of Laws of 1956.

GOVERNMENT

The state of Liberia was founded in 1847 by immigrants of African descent who returned from the United States to their native continent. Liberia has remained an independent nation and is the oldest republic with a president, senate and lower house, although in recent years, there had been considerable domestic upheaval resulting in a revolution in 1990.

INVESTMENT PROFILE

Liberia is a "grand-daddy" of corporate jurisdictions. The Liberian non-resident corporation has been in active international use since 1948. The Liberian Business Corporation Act, adopted in 1977, was modeled on the state corporate laws of Delaware and New York and expanded the original Liberian Corporation Law of 1948.

Not only is there no income tax on a Liberian corporation owned by Liberian non-residents, but there is total secrecy simply because there is no requirement to file any information with the government—not even a list of directors. Existence can be obtained in one day. The only information needed is the corporate name, the authorized share capital and the number of directors on the initial board. Privacy is maintained by the beneficial owner throughout the incorporation process and the corporate structure allows complete freedom of operation.

TAXATION

Liberia has treaties with Germany and Sweden to avoid double taxation. Non-resident Liberian corporations do not incur tax liabilities in Liberia if the income is derived from non-Liberian sources.

LIECHTENSTEIN

AT A GLANCE...

Capital
Vaduz

Commercial Center
Vaduz

Location
Liechtenstein is located between Switzerland and Austria.

Climate
The climate is similar to the northeastern United States.

Population
The population is 29,000.

Language
The languages are German and Alemanni.

Currency
The unit of currency is the Swiss Franc.

Communications
Communications are excellent.

OVERVIEW

The financial condition of Liechtenstein is excellent—no national debt, stable political conditions and an absence of political tensions.

Tax legislation is extremely favorable for holding companies. It is a highly industrialized nation with a healthy economy and a firm belief in the principles of free enterprise. Its banks provide secrecy regarding foreign accounts, and all tax matters are treated with a high degree of confidentiality.

This is not to say, however, that Liechtenstein provides an atmosphere of "wheeling and dealing" for individuals and families seeking tax avoidance.

LEGAL SYSTEM

In civil law, Liechtenstein conforms in part to both the Austrian and Swiss systems. Liechtenstein codified a company law in 1926 that is highly regarded as one of the most modem in Europe. Many regulations on legal procedure guarantee the impartiality and fairness of the law.

GOVERNMENT

The government of Liechtenstein is a constitutional monarchy based on democratic and parlimentary procedures that encompass all the principles and practices of a modem government.

Liechtenstein governs on the principle of separation of powers where legislation, administration and court actions are concerned.

INVESTMENT PROFILE

Liechtenstein recognizes a variety of enterprises and company forms. The most suitable forms to be used as holding companies are the *anstalt* (establishment), the *akteigesellschift* (company limited by shares), and the registered trust. Liechtenstein has designed legislation that is particularly favorable to the protection and administration of financial structures.

Liechtenstein tax legislation defines holding companies as enterprises that exclusively administer capital or assets such as shares or bonds of other enterprises.

If a holding or domiciled company is formed as a legal personality and is entered into the public registry, it will have special tax privileges:

- Tax exemptions on all assets and income
- Reduction of the capital tax
- Exemption from all taxes on profits and earnings
- Reduction of the formation stamp duty
- A further reduction of the capital tax for the foundation with high capital
- Absolute secrecy regarding tax matters

TAXATION

Liechtenstein levies no income taxes against any company that is domiciled there if the company does not receive Liechtenstein source income. There are low registration and annual capital taxes on such companies.

Bearer shares are permitted but foreign banks and mutual funds are not.

The top rate for personal income taxes in Liechtenstein is 7.5 percent. The taxes on company profits vary from 5 to 12 percent, in accordance with a ratio of profit to net worth. People who are considered residents of Liechtenstein for tax purposes, must pay taxes on all income from gainful activity that is derived from a partnership, membership or proprietorship of any enterprise that has an office registered in Liechtenstein.

Foreigners and Liechtenstein nationals who have their permanent residence in a foreign country are not required to pay taxes on income derived this way. Such persons also are exempt from property taxes on the share of an enterprise that they might hold. Liechtenstein has a double taxation agreement with Austria but with no other country.

LUXEMBOURG

AT A GLANCE...

Capital
Luxembourg City

Commercial Center
Luxembourg City

Location
Luxembourg adjoins Belgium, France, and Germany.

Climate
The climate is similar to the northeastern United States.

Population
The population is 375,000.

Language
The languages are Letzeburgesh, French, German and English.

Currency
The unit of currency is the Luxembourg franc.

Communications
Communications are excellent. By air, Luxembourg is only an hour from Germany, France and Great Britain.

OVERVIEW

Offshore investment has become more attractive in Luxembourg primarily because of the absence of withholding tax on the interest of European bond issues.

The investor should keep in mind that in Luxembourg, a secrecy law violation is considered to be only a civil offense and that this country cannot offer the almost guaranteed privacy of many other investment centers.

LEGAL SYSTEM

German, Belgian and French judicial customs and law make up the Luxembourg judicial system.

GOVERNMENT

The government of Luxembourg is a constitutional monarchy. Control of the government is evenly divided between the monarch, the cabinet and the elected legislative wing. Luxembourg gained independence in 1839.

INVESTMENT PROFILE

Luxembourg is well suited as a tax haven for specific purposes. Luxembourg legislation is designed to attract holding companies.

There are two types of holding companies in Luxembourg: The mixed-holding company and the pure-holding company.

The mixed holding company is one that administers an investment portfolio, takes participating interests, develops patents and engages in direct industrial/commercial activity. Tax advantages do not apply to the mixed-holding company.

A pure holding company is one whose sole object is the taking of participating interests in other Luxembourg or foreign undertakings and the administering of these participating interests.

The company cannot carry on any industrial activity or maintain a commercial establishment open to the public. The establishment of a pure holding company can result in a considerably reduced expense budget for a corporation.

Consider the following:

- Regardless of a company's profits, there is only a single, small annual tax.
- The liberal judicial system of Luxembourg is geared toward the needs of the holding company.
- All the principals of a company, such as the promoters, directors, auditors and managers may be of any foreign nationality and may reside in other countries.
- The law does not require the publication of the list of company securities.
- Luxembourg revenue authorities do not examine or supervise the books of holding companies.

TAXATION

Generally, since Luxembourg pure-holding companies are not really being doubly taxed, they are not qualified for a reduced withholding tax. There is no taxation on the proceeds of liquidations, and there are no communal taxes. There is no Luxembourg tax levied against dividends distributed by a pure-holding company, either against the company itself or against foreign shareholders.

No tax is levied against coupons of foreign securities, such as shares and bonds, that are held by a pure-holding company.

Luxembourg has double-taxation treaties with Austria, Belgium, Brazil, Denmark, Finland, France, Germany, Iceland, Ireland, Italy, Korea, Morocco, the Netherlands, Norway, Spain, Sweden, the United Kingdom and the United States.

MALTA

AT A GLANCE...

Capital
Valetta

Commercial Center
Valetta

Location
Malta consists of five islands located between Gibraltar and Suez.

Climate
The climate is typically Mediterranean with mild winters and sunny summers.

Population
The population is approximately 350,000.

Language
The languages are English, Maltese, Italian and French. Business is conducted in English.

Currency
The currency is the Maltese lira. There are no exchange control restrictions that apply to offshore companies.

Communications
Communications are excellent.

Malta is within easy reach of major European and Middle-Eastern business centers and is in the same time zone as Frankfurt, Milan, Paris and Zurich. By air, Malta is three hours from London and Frankfurt, two hours from Paris and one hour from Rome. A full satellite direct-dialing system connects Malta with most parts of the world through a 2,000 port international exchange.

OVERVIEW

Malta has a tradition of being fiercely independent and neutral over a period of many centuries.

It is strategically located in the western Mediterranean and historically has been a staging post, trading point, supply center and military base. Today, Malta has a profitable manufacturing sector and a thriving tourist industry as well as being a hub of shipbuilding and ship repair.

Since 1989, Malta has offered a wide range of tax and financial benefits to banks, insurance companies, insurance managers, fund managers, trading companies, holding and personal investment companies, pension funds, ship owners and trusts.

Trading companies are expected to have a physical and functional presence on the island because Malta wants to establish itself as a reputable international financial center.

LEGAL SYSTEM

Malta's judiciary is long established and independent. Its laws are based on Roman law and the Napoleonic Code while more recent fiscal, company and shipping laws are based on English statute law.

GOVERNMENT

Malta is a sovereign European state with a democratic parliamentary system based on the British model. It is a member of the Commonwealth, and its first self-governing constitution dates back to 1921.

INVESTMENT PROFILE

The island has had an association agreement with the European Community since 1971. It has a large network of diplomatic ties, double taxation treaties, and commercial and investment protection agreements.

Non-trading companies may opt for nondisclosure of shareholders and directors. Registration is possible in the name of local nominees. The law provides for the protection of this privacy in legal proceedings. Such companies need not have their accounts audited or file an annual return or a copy of their accounts with the government.

Non-trading companies include:

- Corporate and personal holding companies.
- Companies that limit their activities to the ownership, management and administration of property of any kind.
- Shipping companies which own and operate ships registered under any flag.

TAXATION

Trading companies are liable for a five-percent tax. Non-trading companies are completely exempt from income tax. Trusts pay a small fixed annual tax in lieu of a registration fee.

No tax is chargeable on any dividend or interest paid by a trading company or a non-trading company. In fact, there are no withholding, capital gains or other taxes.

MONACO

AT A GLANCE...

Capital
Monaco-Villa

Commercial Center
Monaco-Villa

Location
Monaco is located on the French Riviera.

Climate
Monaco has a mild climate.

Population
The population is 29,000.

Language
The languages are French, English, Italian and Monegasque.

Currency
The unit of currency is the French franc.

Communications
Communications are excellent.

OVERVIEW

Monaco offers a variety of international banking services. Numbered bank accounts are unavailable and non-resident bank deposits are able to be transferred to the currency of choice. However, the postal authorities or properly authorized banks oversee foreign exchange transactions.

LEGAL SYSTEM

Monaco law is based on the French civil code.

GOVERNMENT

Monaco is an independent sovereignty and the government is a constitutional monarchy headed by Prince Rainier III.

INVESTMENT PROFILE

Prior government approval is required to incorporate a foreign company branch. Three years of audited statements as well as other documents must be submitted. To organize a Societe Anonyme Monegasque (SAM), certain guidelines must be followed:

- A minimum of two share-holders and two directors are required.
- One director must be a legal resident.
- Minimum capitalization is needed.
- Issued-in-kind shares cannot be traded for two years although registered and bearer shares are allowed.
- Within 15 days of incorporation, the company must be registered with the Official List of Companies.
- The headquarters of the corporation must be located within Monaco.
- A company auditor must be appointed, and the auditor must be a registered chartered accountant.

TAXATION

Companies with a quarter of their income from sources outside of Monaco would be subject to profit tax. A 35 percent tax is collected on net profits for local and foreign companies.

Interest, dividends, capital gains, gifts, inheritance, transfer of real estate, commissions and royalties are taxed. Profit taxes are levied on companies that derive income from processes, formulas and intellectual property rights.

Monaco does have a tax treaty with France but with no other country at this time.

MONTSERRAT

AT A GLANCE...

Capital
Plymouth

Commercial Center
Plymouth

Location
Montserrat is an island located in the Eastern Caribbean. Its nearest neighbors are Nevis and Antigua.

Climate
The climate ranges from 70°F to 80°F.

Population
The population is approximately 13,000.

Language
The official language is English.

Currency
The unit of currency is the Eastern Caribbean dollar.

Communications
Communications are excellent.

OVERVIEW

Montserrat, due to several money-laundering scandals in the '80s should not be used for banking.

While the government is revamping its banking system, there is a moratorium on new bank charters.

LEGAL SYSTEM

The legal system is based on English common law and has an independent judicial system.

GOVERNMENT

Montserrat is a British dependency.

INVESTMENT PROFILE

Certain suggestions were made by the Gallagher Report for the revising of offshore banking procedure in Montserrat.

Among the suggestions: only internationally recognized, financially solid banks should do business in Montserrat. Rules for an International Business Company are as follows:

- One director is required, and both the directors and the shareholders can be of any nationality.
- There must be a registered office in Montserrat.
- There is a minimum of one shareholder, and an IBC is limited by shares.

TAXATION

Montserrat has tried to encourage offshore business with the tax-free IBC. To qualify for up to 15 tax-free years of operation, the business must manufacture approved products and be in an approved business category.

Montserrat has double-taxation agreements with a variety of countries but not with the United States.

NETHERLANDS

AT A GLANCE...

Capital
Amsterdam

Commercial Center
Amsterdam

Location
The Netherlands borders the North Sea and is located between Germany and Belgium.

Climate
The climate of the Netherlands remains fairly cold year round with temperatures rarely exceeding 70°F.

Population
The population of the Netherlands is approximately 15 million.

Language
The official language is Dutch.

Currency
The unit of currency is the Dutch guilder.

Communications
Communications are excellent.

OVERVIEW

The Netherlands is an established tax haven that allows substantial tax benefits to companies formed for specific business purposes.

However, the internal tax structure of the Netherlands is comparable to other heavily taxed nations.

LEGAL SYSTEM

Civil and penal law are the basis of the legal system.

GOVERNMENT

The kingdom of the Netherlands is a constitutional monarchy with a democratic parliamentary government. By this means, the monarch, government and parliament together rule the country.

INVESTMENT PROFILE

The Netherlands should not be considered as a tax haven country in any general sense. However, it does offer considerable advantages to holding and finance companies. In the appropriate circumstances, formation of a Dutch company could be used to finance other companies in a group and at the same time function as a holding company.

There are three types of companies that benefit from the Netherlands tax legislation: the finance subsidiary, the holding company and the participating company.

The finance subsidiary is primarily active in the financing of the operation of the foreign parent or other closely related companies through the use of Euro-currency loans. The finance subsidiary will escape any restriction on the debt-to-equity ratio as long as the finance subsidiary borrows funds from, and lends funds to, non-resident affiliate companies. Interest paid on bonds, notes and other debt obligations are not subject to any Netherlands withholding tax. Interest paid by the finance subsidiary is deductible as an expense against the profits of the company. A holding company must be a corporation with virtually no assets other than a majority of shares in other companies and fulfill an essential function within those organizations.

Holding companies are exempt from corporate tax on dividends received by the company. And if the country involved has a tax treaty with the Netherlands, there will be a decrease of the withholding tax at its source.

The participating company must own at least five percent of the outstanding shares of the capital stock of another corporation. To be exempt from corporate income tax on dividends and profits received, the participating company must meet minimum participation qualifications.

TAXATION

The tax haven company should be designed so that it avoids any internal tax liability. Tax exemptions are provided within the Netherlands on specific qualifying activities, and there are treaties maintained by the government to avoid double taxation.

NETHERLANDS ANTILLES

AT A GLANCE...

Capital
Willemstad

Commercial Center
Willemstad

Location
The Antilles are made up of the Leeward Islands and the Windward Islands which are approximately 500 miles apart. The Windward Islands are east of Puerto Rico and the Leeward Islands are north of Venezuela.

Climate
The climate is hot and humid most of the year.

Population
The population is 190,000.

Language
The languages are Dutch, English, Spanish and Papiamento.

Currency
The unit of currency is the Netherlands Antilles guilder.

Communications
Communications are excellent.

OVERVIEW

In the past 30 years, offshore banking has grown into a booming industry for the Netherlands Antilles. However, stringent standards do limit all but the most determined bankers from setting up shop. Money brought into the Antilles is not subject to exchange controls.

LEGAL SYSTEM

The Antilles has a civil system based on that of the Netherlands.

GOVERNMENT

The government is based on the parliamentary system of the Netherlands and is self-governing but still a part of the Netherlands.

INVESTMENT PROFILE

There are a substantial number of foreign corporations in the Antilles today primarily because the Antilles offers an attractive corporate package.

Shareholders may appoint one or more managing directors. The shareholders appoint at least one managing director (an individual or corporation). If the managing agent is the sole director, that party must be a resident or corporation of the Netherlands Antilles. Annual financial statements do not need to be filed with the commercial register for most companies. It takes approximately two weeks for a corporation to become a legal entity. Here's how it works:

The company is incorporated by one person and a deed is drawn up, notarized, and then submitted to the minister of justice for approval. Shares are conveyed to the owners after incorporation.

TAXATION

Certain income-tax exemptions make the Antilles a very attractive tax-haven package. For instance, income-tax exemption may be given for as many as 11 years if a company can show it "significantly" contributes to the economy of the Antilles. No tax is paid on the income of companies that collect capital gains, royalties and dividends. Holding companies pay up to a three-percent tax on net income.

NEVIS

AT A GLANCE...

Capital
Basseterre

Commercial Center
Basseterre

Location
Nevis is located in the Leeward Islands approximately 1,200 miles southeast of Miami.

Climate
The climate is nearly perfect and the variation in altitude and soil conditions creates a natural garden of tropical vegetation.

Population
The current population is 8,000 with 35,000 residents living in the neighboring island of St. Kitts.

Language
English is the official and commercial language of the island.

Currency
The official unit of currency is the Eastern Caribbean dollar. There are no currency exchange controls.

Communications
Nevis offers excellent communication facilities which include direct dialing to the U.S., Canada and Europe as well as worldwide telex, facsimile and telegraph services. Direct airline service is available to most major cities in North America and Europe.

OVERVIEW

Nevis offers a very attractive package for the offshore investor. No taxes are levied in Nevis on income, dividends or distribution of a Nevis company which are not earned on the island. Corporate financial returns, annual reports, and changes of shareholders, directors or officers need not be filed. Shareholders, directors and officers may be of any nationality and reside anywhere. The secretary may be a corporate entity or an individual and companies may serve as directors.

Company records and the principle office may be located anywhere and immediate incorporation is available. Nevis companies may amend their articles of incorporation, merge or consolidate with foreign or other Nevis companies or file articles of dissolution.

LEGAL SYSTEM

The 1983 constitution provides for a federal parliament headed officially by the governor-general. A cabinet in Nevis is lead by the premier as leader of the majority party in the house of assembly. The legal system in the island is based upon English common law, served by a high court of justice and a court of appeal.

GOVERNMENT

Nevis was a British colony from 1628 until 1983 when it became independent and joined the federation of St. Kitts-Nevis. The federation is an active member of the British Commonwealth.

Nevis is a democracy based upon the British parliamentary system and has an elected local assembly.

INVESTMENT PROFILE

The Nevis Business Corporation Ordinance of 1984 governs the establishment of non-resident domestic companies. The ordinance is based upon Delaware and New York laws. However, the ordinance also contains many features of British company law.

A Nevis corporation must have a registered agent in Nevis. The minimum number of directors is three except where the number of shareholders is fewer than three. If that is the case, the number of

directors must be equal to but not less than the number of shareholders.

All documents tiled with the registrar of companies are available for public inspection. However, it is not necessary to file the names of the directors, officers and shareholders.

TAXATION

Offshore companies are exempt from all forms of Nevis taxation. Local companies are liable for a 50-percent tax on profits unless a tax concession has been granted. The Federation of St. Kitts and Nevis has double-taxation treaties with Denmark, New Zealand, Norway, Sweden, Switzerland and the United Kingdom.

PANAMA

AT A GLANCE...

Capital
Panama City

Commercial Center
Panama City

Location
The Republic of Panama is located between Costa Rica and Colombia and forms the narrowest and lowest portion of the isthmus that links North and South America.

Climate
The climate is characterized by humidity and heavy rains. The dry season is from mid-December to the end of April.

Population
The population is approximately 2.3 million.

Language
Spanish is the official language, but many of the people in Panama City and

Colon speak English.

Currency

The local Balboa is on par with the U.S. dollar and exchanges freely with it. All paper money is American. The lack of exchange controls implies that the government does not regulate the money supply.

Communications

Airlines operating through the International Airport provide service to all major cities in North, Central and South America as well as Europe. International telephone, telex, fax and other telecommunications services are excellent. Cristobal, Balboa and certain other ports in the country have facilities for shipping cargo and for accommodating regular ocean-going freighters and passenger ships.

OVERVIEW

Panama is widely used by corporations as a base for their foreign operations. It is notable for the combination of tax and business advantages it offers despite the U.S. invasion in 1991. Such tax and business advantages include:

- No exchange controls, federal reserve or central bank.
- No taxes and no required financial or other annual reports by corporations doing business exclusively outside Panama.
- Relatively low incorporation and annual maintenance costs.
- Privacy guaranteed with both bearer shares and numbered bank accounts in the currency of the depositor's choice with tax-free interest.

- Investing in the shipping industry with minimal governmental fees.
- The prospect of doing business through the Colon Free Zone, duty-free and almost tax-free.
- A tradition of being a tax haven.

Location is the one of the main keys to Panama's popularity as a business center. It is the link between North and South America which includes the famous Panama Canal that connects the Atlantic and Pacific oceans. Panama, until recently, has been a dictatorship run by whomever happens to be in charge of the army, but since the United States invasion, the democratic process seems to be functioning again. However, the military leaders never seemed to tinker with the tax and corporate laws. There is economic freedom unaffected by political turnover.

LEGAL SYSTEM

The legal system is essentially based on civil law. The basic statutes are the constitution, the civil code and the commercial code. Corporate law is based on the Delaware laws of 1927 without amendments.

GOVERNMENT

Panama was a Spanish colony until 1821 when it then became part of the Gran Colombia of Simon Bolivar. In 1903, Panama broke its alliance with Colombia and became an independent republic.

The executive branch of the government is presently composed of a president and two vice presidents elected for a five-year term in 1989 by direct election.

INVESTMENT PROFILE

Incorporation and company maintenance are not expensive in Panama. Panamanian companies that deal exclusively outside Panama keep no financial records locally and are not required to submit any annual financial reports with the local tax authorities.

A stock-register book must be kept for registered stock and a minute book for meetings of shareholders. Stockholder meetings, if not held in Panama, must be officially sanctioned by the Panamanian consul in the country where they are held and then registered in the minute book in Panama. If a Panamanian corporation is not in any way directly involved in domestic business activities in Panama, no annual report has to be made.

TAXATION

Panamanian tax is restricted to Panama sources so that no corporation is taxed on income originating outside Panama. If dividends are paid to stockholders residing outside of Panama, no withholding tax applies, provided the profit underlying the dividends is all derived from sources outside of Panama.

No inheritance taxes apply if the property inherited is owned by a Panamanian corporation and the assets themselves are outside Panama.

Panama has no double-taxation agreements.

PHILIPPINES

AT A GLANCE...

Capital
Manila

Commercial Center
Manila and Quezan City

Location
The Philippine islands are an archipelago of more than 7,000 islands located approximately 500 miles from the southeast coast of Asia.

Climate
The climate is hot and humid with temperatures ranging from 70°F to 100°F.

Population
The population is 64.6 million.

Language
English is widely spoken for business.

Currency
The unit of currency is the peso.

Communications
Communications are excellent.

OVERVIEW

In an effort to bolster the local economy, the Philippines has enacted legislation that incorporates certain restrictions which may ultimately make the Philippines of little value as a tax haven.

The essence of Decree 218 states that any regional headquarters organized in the Philippines that are managed and controlled from outside the country, and do not derive local income, may be entitled to a 100-percent tax exemption. This means that the parent company must be extremely careful to segregate and limit the functions of the regional office.

LEGAL SYSTEM

The supreme court is the highest court and consists of the chief justice and 14 associate judges—all appointed by the president. Each city has its own court.

GOVERNMENT

In 1987, the Philippines established a constitution based on a 24-seat senate and a 250-seat House of Representatives with the president serving a six-year term.

INVESTMENT PROFILE

In order to set up an office or company in the Philippines, the following must be met:

- A Filipino commercial attache or a consul must present certification to the government that the foreign firm is a legal entity engaged in international trade with affiliates, subsidiaries or regional offices in the Asia-Pacific area.
- A principal officer of the multinational firm must present certification to the Filipino government stating that the multinational firm has been authorized by its board of directors to establish regional offices in the Philippines. This certification must state that the regional office will act only in a supervisory, coordinating or communications capacity for its affiliates, subsidiaries and branches in the Asia-Pacific area.
- The multinational firm must agree to spend at least U.S. $50,000 annually to cover the expenses of its operation in the Philippines.

TAXATION

Tax exemptions are granted to a regional office if the following qualifications are met:

- It is exempt from Section 191— three percent on gross receipts of contractors, proprietors or operations of dockyards and other activates.
- It has an 100-percent exemption from all income tax in the Philippines.
- It is exempt from all licenses, fees and local taxes.
- Its executive personnel qualify for a reduction of the normal withholding tax that is applicable to their wages. The normal tax is 30 percent which is reduced to 15 percent.
- There are no import duties on equipment necessary to maintain the local office or on household items of foreign personnel who manage the office. Furthermore, normal immigration requirements are relaxed so that foreign personnel may have free movement into the Philippines. The normal corporate tax rate of the Philippines is 35 percent on taxable income with foreign branches and resident corporations paying an additional 20 percent on profits remitted abroad.

PUERTO RICO

AT A GLANCE...

Capital
San Juan

Commercial Center
San Juan

Location.
Puerto Rico is located in the Caribbean Sea about 1,000 miles southeast of Florida.

Climate
The climate is mild with an average temperature of 77°F.

Population
The population is approximately 3.5 million.

Language
The languages are Spanish and English.

Currency
The unit of currency is the U.S. dollar.

Communications
Communications are excellent. Puerto Rico is part of the U.S. postal system and domestic postage rates apply to mail between the U.S. and Puerto Rico. U.S. citizens do not need a passport to travel to Puerto Rico. San Juan has become a major air-transportation hub for the region. Miami is two and one-half hours by plane.

OVERVIEW

Puerto Rico is a United States controlled tax haven in the enviable position of enjoying the advantages that an alliance with the U.S. can bring, but with an internal tax system that is separate and distinct from that of the U.S.

Puerto Rico has traditionally been able to offer substantial tax haven benefits to corporations. Puerto Rican corporations also are eligible for U.S. government aid programs such as employment training and loans from the Economic Development Administration.

Puerto Rico's access to the Latin American consumer market together with its unique tax advantages, places the corporate office in an enviable regional position.

LEGAL SYSTEM

The supreme court is the highest court in Puerto Rico. Seven justices are appointed by a governor and serve until they are 70.

GOVERNMENT

Puerto Rico is a self-governing part of the United States and has a good deal of control over internal affairs. Puerto Rican citizen cannot vote in national elections but can vote in national primary elections.

INVESTMENT PROFILE

Mail order companies, publishers, consultants, service firms and many others who are looking to explore the Latin American market, should find a Puerto Rican-based enterprise to be profitable.

The Puerto Rican trade zones offer business possibilities. These trade zones, which are outside the U.S. Customs territory, rent such facilities as warehouse and assembly space—important assets for a company working in the Latin American market. Coupled with the export-manufacturing exemption, this provides a tax-free and duty-free base of operations within the jurisdiction of the United States.

Another bonus: Equipment, supplies, and goods can be transferred from the U.S. mainland without duties because Puerto Rico is treated as any other state.

TAXATION

Puerto Rico is not a part of the U.S. for income tax purposes. Therefore, it considers U.S. source income as foreign source income. Puerto Rico does not tax foreign source income of a foreign company that has a branch in Puerto Rico. A Puerto Rican branch could be used for the company's international business and only the income actually earned in Puerto Rico would be subject to Puerto Rican taxation.

SINGAPORE

AT A GLANCE...

Capital
Singapore

Commercial Center
Singapore

Location
Singapore is located south of Thailand.

Climate
The climate is hot and humid for most of the year.

Population
The population is 2.6 million.

Language
The languages are English, Chinese, Tamil and Malay with English being the official language.

Currency
The unit of currency is the Singapore dollar.

Communications
Communications are excellent.

OVERVIEW

Singapore is a leader in the financial world of Asia and attracts foreign investors from all over the world. The government offers specific incentives for companies to resettle in Singapore and multinational companies are encouraged to set up headquarters as well.

Because Singapore is in the "hub" of Southeast Asia, it is ideal for all types of businesses. There are many high-tech companies located in Singapore, attracted by the excellent labor and government incentives.

LEGAL SYSTEM

The Singapore legal system is based on the British model.

GOVERNMENT

In 1965, Singapore declared itself an independent country. The government is made up of the executive, legislative and judicial branches. The ceremonial president is elected by a unicameral parliament, and the prime minister and cabinet have executive power.

INVESTMENT PROFILE

Private limited companies require low start-up fees and only two shareholders. However, one shareholder and the company secretary must be residents and in a private company, share transfer is limited.

Non-residents can open high-interest accounts from certain Singapore banks and numbered bank accounts are available.

TAXATION

Singapore does not tax passive income by resident and non-resident shareholders in Singapore corporations. Services originating and income earned outside of Singapore are not taxed on profits or capital gains.

Foreign income deposits do not pay withholding taxes and dividends also are not taxable. Singapore has tax treaties with many different nations but not with the United States.

ST. VINCENT

AT A GLANCE...

Capital
Kingstown

Commercial Center
Kingstown

Location
St. Vincent is part of the Windward Islands and is located west of Barbados.

Climate
The climate is hot and humid.

Population
The population is approximately 110,000.

Language
The languages are English and French patois.

Currency
The unit of currency is the Eastern Caribbean dollar.

Communications
Communications are excellent.

OVERVIEW

Offshore companies, such as banks, corporations, hotels and resorts, will find very favorable legislation in St. Vincent. In addition, eligible exporters receive 15 years of tax-free business

LEGAL SYSTEM

English common law is the basis of the legal system primarily because St. Vincent is a former British colony.

GOVERNMENT

St. Vincent is a democracy. The prime minister has executive power and a governor-general represents the Queen.

INVESTMENT PROFILE

The International Companies Act regulates offshore companies. The following applies to offshore companies:

- Incorporation for limited-liability offshore companies is done by filing articles of association and the memorandum of association with the St. Vincent Trust Authority.
- No minimum capital is required.
- Three directors are necessary for incorporation.
- International companies not doing business locally are not subject to local tax.
- The company name must end with "limited."
- Anonymity for beneficial owners is guaranteed through nominee subscribers.

TAXATION

An international company is responsible for company registration fees but not for taxes on income that does not originate in St. Vincent.

St. Vincent has approximately 60 double-taxation agreements with other countries.

SWITZERLAND

AT A GLANCE...

Capital
Bern

Commercial Center
Zurich

Location
Switzerland is located in central Europe and borders Italy, Austria, Germany, France and Liechtenstein.

Climate
The climate is much like the northeastern United States.

Population
The population is approximately seven million.

Language
Switzerland is multilingual: German, French, Italian and Romansch are all official languages. The business community uses English and French.

Currency
The unit of currency is the Swiss franc.

Communications
Communications are excellent. Switzerland boasts excellent internal roads and railways. It also is accessible by river barge directly from the sea. Airline service is excellent, and telecommunications are the best available.

OVERVIEW

The Swiss federal constitution guarantees an economic system based upon the principles of free trade and commerce. Since World War II, Switzerland has developed into one of the world's foremost financial centers primarily by strengthening its financial position in the various fields of international capital exchange. Its development as a financial fortress is evidenced by its now favorable international investment position.

LEGAL SYSTEM

The legal system is grounded in the civil-law tradition.

GOVERNMENT

Switzerland is politically stable and this is reflected in its history, legal structure and present socioeconomic situation. Its basic constitution, enacted in 1848 and revised in 1974, gives the country a confederation system. The foreign policy for centuries has been peaceful neutrality concerning all international conflicts.

INVESTMENT PROFILE

Switzerland has a well developed system of banking that is responsible for a large portion of foreign assets and liabilities. By the nature of most business conducted in Switzerland, its banks are forced to compete with international banks. Their success is largely attributable to the soundness of the Swiss franc.

Switzerland is not a good place for a holding company. Swiss incorporation is expensive and taxes are relatively high. The one exception can be found in the Canton of Neuchatel which offers special tax reductions of up to ten years for both manufacturing and service businesses—particularly high-tech industries. Each case is handled on an individual basis, but they are generally liberal in granting the concession and also can recommend residence visas and work permits be granted to company managers.

TAXATION

Switzerland has a somewhat complex system of federal taxation. Due to its federal structure, taxes are levied concurrently by three different authorities: the federal government, the cantons and the municipalities. Swiss federal tax laws are uniform throughout the country but the laws of the cantons and municipalities may differ.

All taxes on worldwide income add up to approximately 25 to 35 percent, clearly showing that Switzerland is no tax haven. On the surface, the extensive Swiss network of double-taxation treaties would seem to offer relief from the heavy taxes. The treaties usually reduce the withholding taxes to 15 percent or 20 percent. However, the Swiss government has taken special measures to restrict the usability of the agreements for tax-minimalization purposes.

TURKS & CAICOS

AT A GLANCE...

Capital
Grand Turk

Commercial Center
Grand Turk

Location
The Turks and Caicos are north of Haiti and the Dominican Republic and are at the bottom of the Bahama islands chain.

Climate
The climate is hot and humid.

Population
The population is 9,500.

Language
The official language is English.

Currency
The unit of currency is the U.S. dollar.

Communications
Communications are excellent.

OVERVIEW

Thanks to the New Company Act of 1982, the Turks and Caicos enjoy a burgeoning foreign investment.

Until new legislation is drafted, the Turks and Caicos may be closed to all but branches or subsidiaries of reputable international banks.

LEGAL SYSTEM

The legal system is based on English common law.

GOVERNMENT

The Turks and Caicos are a self-governing British Crown colony.

INVESTMENT PROFILE

There are two kinds of companies that can be set up in the islands but it is the exempt company that is set up to handle off-shore investment.

The exempt company has some very attractive advantages:

- There is no minimum authorized capital:
- A business license is not required.
- Officers, directors and members do not have to be identified.
- Incorporation takes three days.
- There are no requirements that

capital be in a certain currency.

- Par value is not required for a company purchasing its own shares and can be set at any sum.

The Turks and Caicos simplifies stockholding. Registered stock may be held by just one person who may hold the position of both director and secretary. Bearer shares are also allowed to be issued.

TAXATION

No double-taxation treaties are held with any other country.

Inheritance, income, sales, capital gains, gift, succession, property and dividend taxes do not apply in the Turks and Caicos.

VANUATU

AT A GLANCE...

Capital
Port Vila

Commercial Center
Port Vila

Location
Vanuatu is a group of islands located in the South Pacific approximately 1,400 off the coast of Australia.

Climate
The climate is hot and humid all year.

Population
The population is approximately 150,000.

Language
The languages are Melanesian, French and English.

Currency
The unit of currency is the Vatu, and there are no exchange controls.

Communications
Communications are excellent.

OVERVIEW

The government promotes Vanuatu as a financial center, encouraging offshore corporate, bank, insurance and trust formations. Commercial banking services are available.

LEGAL SYSTEM

The legal system is based on English common law.

GOVERNMENT

The independent republic government is a parliamentary democracy with a judicial, legislative and executive branch headed by an elected president.

INVESTMENT PROFILE

The companies used for off-shore business are the exempt company and the private company.

In the exempt company:
- Disclosure of beneficial owners is not required.
- The law requires that secrecy be maintained.
- Audits are not required.
- Documents and returns are not public record.
- A public offering cannot be made by the company.

In the private company:
- The maximum number of

shareholders allowed is 50.
- Two shareholders and at least one director, are required.
- Nominee shareholders are not necessary.
* Transfer of shares is restricted.

TAXATION

There are no capital gains or income tax in Vanuatu.

WESTERN SAMOA

AT A GLANCE...

Capital
Apia

Commercial Center
Apia

Location
Western Samoa is comprised of two large islands and seven smaller islands and is situated in the center of the Southern Pacific Ocean between Honolulu and Sydney and east of the International Date Line. The island of Upola is the most developed island.

Climate
The climate is tropical and temperatures range between 75°F to 85°F.

Population
The population of the islands is approximately 162,000.

Language
English is widely spoken and is taught in all schools.

Currency
The unit of currency is the Tala and currently, there are no currency exchange controls.

Communications
Western Samoa has an excellent international telecommunications system with telex, facsimile and international direct-dialing facilities via satellite. A modem airport provides direct access to New Zealand, Australia, Fiji, the Cook Islands and Hawaii. The country is well serviced by Pacific region shipping services.

OVERVIEW
Western Samoa has a long history of social, political and economic stability. Modern offshore legislation gives great flexibility for the offshore company and an established domestic banking system provides proven international connections. Western Samoa has a well-developed economic and commercial infrastructure and offers immediate company availability.

Principals of international companies may remain anonymous. There is no obligation to discuss details of beneficial ownership. Such anonymity is guaranteed by law.

LEGAL SYSTEM
The Western Samoan superior court possesses and exercises all the jurisdiction, power and authority necessary to administer the laws of Western Samoa. The Western Samoan court of appeals hears appeals on any judgment, decree or order of the supreme court in either its civil or criminal jurisdiction.

GOVERNMENT
Western Samoa has been a fully independent nation since 1962 and its constitution provides for a parliamentary

government which combines the traditional Samoan social structure and a democratic voting system.

There is a 47-member legislative assembly which consists of 45 Matai titleholders who are elected by their peers and two non-Samoan residents who are registered on the Universal Voters Roll. Parliamentary elections are held every three years.

INVESTMENT PROFILE

The International Companies Act of 1987 regulates offshore banking companies. Under this act, companies may be incorporated as international companies or registered as foreign companies if they have been incorporated outside of Western Samoa. The shareholders of these companies must be non-residents of Western Samoa. However, a resident trustee company registered under the Trustee Companies Act of 1987 may hold shares

in international companies.

International companies must maintain proper books of account. However, they are not required to file annual accounts or financial statements. It is not necessary to appoint an auditor unless the company is a licensed bank, registered insurer or is raising funds from the public. Directors and shareholders' meetings may be held anywhere in the world. Only one director need be appointed, and there is no obligation to appoint a resident director. Corporations may be directors. A resident secretary must be appointed and should be an officer or subsidiary of a registered trustee company.

TAXATION

Western Samoa is not a party to any double-taxation agreements. No international offshore company pays taxes.

Whatever you need to know we've made it E-Z!

Informative text and forms you can fill o
on-screen.* From personal to business, leg
to leisure—we've made it E-Z!

PERSONAL & FAMILY

For all your family's needs, we have titles that will help keep you organized and guide you through most every aspect of your personal life.

BUSINESS

Whether you're starting from scratch with a home business or you just want to keep your corporate records in shape, we've got the programs for you.

* Not all topics include forms   ss 1999.r2

	Item#	Qty.	Price Ea.‡
★ **E•Z Legal Kits**			
Bankruptcy	K100		$23.95
Incorporation	K101		$23.95
Divorce	K102		$29.95
Credit Repair	K103		$21.95
Living Trust	K105		$21.95
Living Will	K106		$23.95
Last Will & Testament	K107		$18.95
Buying/Selling Your Home	K111		$21.95
Employment Law	K112		$21.95
Collecting Child Support	K115		$21.95
Limited Liability Company	K116		$21.95
★ **Made E•Z Software**			
Accounting Made E-Z	SW1207		$29.95
Asset Protection Made E-Z	SW1157		$29.95
Bankruptcy Made E-Z	SW1154		$29.95
Best Career Oppportunities Made E-Z	SW1216		$29.95
Brain-Buster Crossword Puzzles	SW1223		$29.95
Brain-Buster Jigsaw Puzzles	SW1222		$29.95
Business Startups Made E-Z	SW1192		$29.95
Buying/Selling Your Home Made E-Z	SW1213		$29.95
Car Buying Made E-Z	SW1146		$29.95
Corporate Record Keeping Made E-Z	SW1159		$29.95
Credit Repair Made E-Z	SW1153		$29.95
Divorce Law Made E-Z	SW1182		$29.95
Everyday Law Made E-Z	SW1185		$29.95
Everyday Legal Forms & Agreements	SW1186		$29.95
Incorporation Made E-Z	SW1176		$29.95
Last Wills Made E-Z	SW1177		$29.95
Living Trusts Made E-Z	SW1178		$29.95
Offshore Investing Made E-Z	SW1218		$29.95
Owning a Franchise Made E-Z	SW1202		$29.95
Touring Florence, Italy Made E-Z	SW1220		$29.95
Touring London, England Made E-Z	SW1221		$29.95
Vital Record Keeping Made E-Z	SW1160		$29.95
Website Marketing Made E-Z	SW1203		$29.95
Your Profitable Home Business	SW1204		$29.95
★ **Made E•Z Guides**			
Bankruptcy Made E-Z	G200		$17.95
Incorporation Made E-Z	G201		$17.95
Divorce Law Made E-Z	G202		$17.95
Credit Repair Made E-Z	G203		$17.95
Living Trusts Made E-Z	G205		$17.95
Living Wills Made E-Z	G206		$17.95
Last Wills Made E-Z	G207		$17.95
Small Claims Court Made E-Z	G209		$17.95
Traffic Court Made E-Z	G210		$17.95
Buying/Selling Your Home Made E-Z	G211		$17.95
Employment Law Made E-Z	G212		$17.95
Collecting Child Support Made E-Z	G215		$17.95
Limited Liability Companies Made E-Z	G216		$17.95
Partnerships Made E-Z	G218		$17.95
Solving IRS Problems Made E-Z	G219		$17.95
Asset Protection Secrets Made E-Z	G220		$17.95
Immigration Made E-Z	G223		$17.95
Buying/Selling a Business Made E-Z	G223		$17.95
★ **Made E•Z Books**			
Managing Employees Made E-Z	BK308		$29.95
Corporate Record Keeping Made E-Z	BK310		$29.95
Vital Record Keeping Made E-Z	BK312		$29.95
Business Forms Made E-Z	BK313		$29.95
Collecting Unpaid Bills Made E-Z	BK309		$29.95
Everyday Law Made E-Z	BK311		$29.95
Everyday Legal Forms & Agreements	BK307		$29.95
★ **Labor Posters**			
Federal Labor Law Poster	LP001		$11.99
State Labor Law Poster (specify state)			$29.95
★ Shipping & Handling*			$
★ **TOTAL OF ORDER****:**			$

ss 1599.r2

Index

P-Y♦♦♦♦